Old and New Nobility

in Aix-en-Provence, 1600–1695

OLD AND NEW NOBILITY IN AIX-EN-PROVENCE 1600–1695

PORTRAIT OF AN URBAN ELITE

DONNA BOHANAN

LOUISIANA STATE UNIVERSITY PRESS
BATON ROUGE AND LONDON

Copyright © 1992 by Louisiana State University Press
Manufactured in the United States of America
First printing
01 00 99 98 97 96 95 94 93 92   5 4 3 2 1

Designer: Rebecca Lloyd Lemna
Typeface: Bembo
Typesetter: G&S Typesetters, Inc.
Printer and binder: Thomson-Shore, Inc.

Library of Congress Cataloging-in-Publication Data
Bohanan, Donna, 1954–
    Old and new nobility in Aix-en-Provence, 1600–1695 : portrait of
an urban elite / Donna Bohanan.
        p.   cm.
    Includes bibliographical references and index.
    ISBN 0-8071-1624-6 (alk. paper)
    1. Aix-en-Provence (France)—Social life and customs.   2. Upper
classes—France—Aix-en-Provence—History—17th century.   3. City
and town life—France—Aix-en-Provence—History—17th century.
    I. Title.
    DC801.A325B5   1992
    306'.094491—dc20   92-6707
                                                                        CIP

Some of the material in Chapters III and VII, respectively, appeared in the author's
articles "Matrimonial Strategies Among Nobles of Seventeenth-Century Aix-en-
Provence," *Journal of Social History,* XIX (1986), and "The Education of Nobles in
Seventeenth-Century Aix-en-Provence," *Journal of Social History,* XX (1987).

The paper in this book meets the guidelines for permanence and durability of the
Committee on Production Guidelines for Book Longevity of the Council on Library
Resources. ∞

For my parents

CONTENTS

ACKNOWLEDGMENTS

This book was seen to completion only because of the very kind advice and assistance of several individuals, and for their support I am most grateful. To no scholar do I owe a greater debt than to Professor J. Russell Major, who has always served as an intellectual inspiration. His understanding of the early modern period has obviously shaped my own; his example has offered me a model of academic excellence to which I can only aspire; and his continued support bolsters me emotionally as well as intellectually. I can never adequately express my appreciation.

Several other scholars made contributions to this project in a variety of ways. Mack Holt, Al Hamscher, Don Bailey, and Ellery Schalk offered much in the way of encouragement and suggestions over the years. Emmanuel Le Roy Ladurie directed me to sources and to changes in approach that opened new areas of inquiry. And I am particularly indebted to Lloyd Moote and Orest Ranum who both, based on a very close and thoughtful reading of the manuscript, provided advice and criticism that sharpened its focus.

I would also like to thank the staffs of the Archives Départementales des Bouches-du-Rhône, the Archives Communales d'Aix-en-Provence, and the Bibliothèque Méjanes, and in particular Charles Foucquart and Elisabeth Martinez, whose kind attention made my days in the Annexe d'Aix of the Archives Départementales much more productive and enjoyable than they might otherwise have been. My time in Aix and my introduction to the French way of life were all the more pleasant and memorable as the result of the friendship and advice of Monica Maza. And for the opportunity to spend time in Aix, I would also like to express my appreciation to Emory University, which awarded me a graduate fellowship, thereby making my research and much more possible. I am thankful to Auburn University for research leave and a grant that proved invaluable in the preparation of this manuscript. And I owe a tremendous debt to my editor, Gerry Anders, who painstakingly edited, corrected, and scrutinized this manuscript.

Finally, I would like to thank my husband, Frank Smith, who heard more about five Aixois families, their marriages, and their inheritance practices than he ever cared to, but who graciously and lovingly allowed me to impose on his knowledge of law and legal history. For this, for his many stylistic criticisms, and for his remarkable ability to keep things in perspective, I am truly grateful. In the end, it was the unfailing love, support, and encouragement of my parents that saw me through this project and much more, and it is with the greatest of affection that I dedicate my book to them.

ABBREVIATIONS

AC, Aix	Archives Communales, Aix
ADBR, Aix, Marseille	Archives Départementales, Bouches-du-Rhône
B. Méjanes	Bibliothèque Méjanes, Aix
B.N.	Bibliothèque Nationale, Paris
BDR	Les Bouches-du-Rhône: Encyclopédie départementale, ed. Paul Masson (17 vols.; Paris 1913–1937)
IAD, Bouches-du-Rhône	Inventaire sommaire des Archives Départementales des Bouches-du-Rhône
M. Arbaud	Musée d'Arbaud, Aix

Old and New Nobility

in Aix-en-Provence, 1600–1695

INTRODUCTION

All historians of early modern France acknowledge important changes in elite society during the sixteenth and seventeenth centuries. They also agree that these changes resulted from the confluence of specific economic, social, and political trends, including the Price Revolution, the growth of an increasingly prosperous middle class, the bureaucratic expansion of the state, the sale of government offices, changes in warfare, and the demographic attrition of the old nobility. But this is where consensus ends. The past several decades have seen tremendous disagreement and debate over the meaning and effects of the changes that came about in elite society.[1] For some historians the sixteenth century witnessed a great "crisis" of the aristocracy, sufficient ultimately to bring about that group's political demise. For others the same period altered the aristocracy in ways that would eventually ensure its survival and its political hegemony. This divergence in interpretation, propelled by an increasingly detailed understanding of historical realities and by new approaches to the past, is both a source of historiographical controversy and the inspiration for this work.

The traditional interpretation portrays the French nobility as an elite that fell victim in the sixteenth century to the Price Revolution and to the economic and social advances of the middle class, which itself was emerging as a bureaucratic nobility, the *noblesse de robe*. Historians holding this view argue that the ascendant, recently en-

---

1. For excellent overviews of this debate and its participants, see James B. Wood, *The Nobility of the Election of Bayeux, 1463–1666: Continuity Through Change* (Princeton, 1980), "Introduction"; and J. H. M. Salmon, "Storm over the *Noblesse*," *Journal of Modern History,* LIII (1981), 242–57.

I

nobled "robe" families maintained a rather different and completely separate existence from the old military aristocracy, the *noblesse d'épée*—the "sword" nobility—which in turn was rapidly becoming a social anachronism. Confident that a broad functional divide separated these two groups of nobles from the start, the "crisis" historians maintain that wealth, marriage patterns, and education further widened the gap between sword and robe: that sixteenth-century inflation and the rise of capitalism brought the financial ruin of the old seigneurial aristocracy; that the older group's exclusive marriage patterns contributed to its demise; and that the sword nobles lost still more ground because their lack of regard for education and letters disqualified them for many of the offices in the growing bureaucracy of the absolutist state. The alleged decline of the old aristocracy has for such historians broad political implications in that it supposedly permitted the expansion of royal authority with little effective opposition; according to Professors Romier, Mousnier, and Bitton, to name a few, the spectrum of social trends just described accompanied the growth of absolutism as early as the sixteenth century.[2]

For more than forty years now, these notions of aristocratic crisis and absolutism in sixteenth-century France have faced challenge. J. Russell Major has suggested that the authority of the Renaissance monarch was still limited by several factors, not the least of which was an ever-powerful and prosperous aristocracy that survived by adapting to new circumstances.[3] Major and other historians have

2. This interpretation of the nobility and the monarchy of sixteenth- and seventeenth-century France comes most notably from Lucien Romier, *Le Royaume de Catherine de Médicis* (2 vols.: Paris, 1922); Pierre de Vaissière, *Gentilshommes campagnards de l'ancienne France* (Paris, 1925); and G. d'Avenel, *La Noblesse française sous Richelieu* (Paris, 1901). More recently these ideas have been developed by Roland Mousnier, Introduction to Roland Mousnier, J. P. Labatut, and Y. Durand, *Problèmes de stratification sociale: Deux Cahiers de la noblesse pour les Etats-Généraux de 1649–1651* (Paris, 1965); and Mousnier, *La Venalité des offices sous Henri IV et Louis XIII* (2d ed.; Paris, 1971). The idea of a separate robe nobility is an important underlying assumption in Mousnier's description of French institutions and society, *The Institutions of France Under the Absolute Monarchy, 1598–1789,* trans. Brian Pearce (2 vols., Chicago, 1979), and it is equally important in Davis Bitton's concise treatment of the decline of the aristocracy, *The French Nobility in Crisis, 1560–1640* (Stanford, 1969).

3. J. Russell Major, "The Renaissance Monarchy: A Contribution to the Periodization of History." *Emory University Quarterly,* XIII (1957), 112–24; Major, "The Crown and the Aristocracy in Renaissance France," *American Historical Review,* LXIX (1964), 631–45; Major, "Noble Income, Inflation, and the Wars of Religion in

criticized also the traditional interpretation as having been conceived without benefit of detailed local evidence—these traditionalists tended to base their negative assessments of the old nobility and their notions of strife between sword and robe on highly impressionistic literary sources. More recently, James B. Wood and Jonathan Dewald have begun to remedy the early neglect of objective data with their very systematic studies of the social and economic circumstances of the nobilities of Bayeux and Rouen, respectively.[4] Wood and Dewald convincingly demonstrate that the crisis interpretation is not applicable to either place, that newer families were assimilated by older families, and that the old nobility was actually revitalized by an influx of new blood, new talents, and new money.

Wood examines the social and economic lives of sword families and newly ennobled (*anoblis*) families in the *élection* of Bayeux. Specifically, he approaches the relations between old and new nobles in terms of relative wealth, levels of indebtedness, officeholding, and intermarriage. His findings contradict many of the old generalizations about aristocratic crisis. As Wood writes, "The traditional division of the early modern nobility into groups of poor old soldiers and new rich officials simply does not apply to the *élection* of Bayeux."[5] He sees old families as leading still-healthy financial lives, participating in officeholding, and marrying regularly with anoblis. Conversely, he shows that in Bayeux there were plenty of impoverished anoblis and that in any case, the anoblis in general tended to abandon offices after attaining noble status. All of this challenges the idea of two separate nobilities, the older in decline. Wood's findings not only contradict the internal-conflict notion, but they also suggest the possibility of a vigorous political life on the part of the nobility as a whole—the kind of political life that in fact occurred during the Wars of Religion.

Wood's discoveries are not unlike those of Dewald, whose study

---

France," *American Historical Review,* LXXXVI (1981), 21–48; Major, *Representative Government in Early Modern France* (New Haven, 1980). See also Mack P. Holt, Introduction to *Society and Institutions in Early Modern France,* ed. Mack P. Holt (Athens, Ga., 1991), xi–xxiii.

4. See Wood, *Nobility of the Election of Bayeux;* and Jonathan Dewald, *The Formation of a Provincial Nobility: The Magistrates of the Parlement of Rouen, 1499–1610* (Princeton, 1980).

5. Wood, *Nobility of the Election of Bayeux,* 158.

of the parlementaires of Rouen also adds substantial detail to the revisionist depiction of the provincial nobility. Not only does Dewald question the idea of conflict between sword and robe, but he even maintains that in Normandy "the *noblesse de robe* grew out of aristocratic society, rather than in opposition to it." He finds many of the parlementaires to have been *créatures* of the court aristocracy—that is, clients or dependents of venerable and powerful houses. In comparing the management of wealth among old and new houses, Dewald detected little difference in strategies or outcomes. Moreover, his findings refute, for this region, the standard interpretation of economic crisis and political decline on the part of the noblesse d'épée.[6] Wood's and Dewald's studies constitute major strides toward a much more accurate and complete understanding of the French nobility. Primary among the two works' many virtues is the fact that they offer richly detailed and largely quantitative information on the social and economic worlds of the provincial nobility. A very different approach appears in the work of Ellery Schalk, who has studied changing images of nobility in an effort to establish a relationship between social, economic, and political realities and the development of new cultural ideals. Using literary sources, Schalk traces the late-sixteenth- and early-seventeenth-century shift in the meaning of "nobility," a shift he describes as leading from the medieval view of nobility as a military function to the more modern perception of the nobility as an elite based on pedigree and refinement. This change in perception allowed the nobility to retain its privileged status following decades of religious and political turmoil during which nobles as a class more or less discredited their claims to privilege on the basis of valor. According to Schalk, this transition in the meaning and nature of nobility had important political reverberations: it accompanied and permitted the emergence of the modern absolutist state. Schalk's major contribution has been to round out the debate between traditionalists and revisionists by addressing cultural changes and the evolution of attitudes about nobility, thereby adding a much-needed cultural dimension to the revisionists' efforts.

This is not to suggest that all work done over the last four decades has been conceived in the revisionist vein, or that all scholars have

6. Dewald, *Formation of a Provincial Nobility*, 15, 309; Ellery Schalk, *From Valor to Pedigree: Ideas of Nobility in France in the Sixteenth and Seventeenth Centuries* (Princeton, 1986).

been converted to the new ways of thinking about nobility. There are still those who, unconvinced, cling to traditional categories of nobility and traditional methods of analysis. In 1968 Davis Bitton offered a restatement, based on literary sources, of the old crisis interpretation. Even more recently, George Huppert has suggested a modified version of the old sword-robe approach to this early modern elite.[7] Huppert prefers to call the anoblis "gentry." He labels them even more descriptively as "les bourgeois gentilshommes," and he is firm in his belief that they were not part of the nobility. In fact, he claims, they were distinctly contemptuous of the sword and deliberately attempted to create a separate culture founded on classical rather than medieval ideals of nobility. Meanwhile, they were similarly detached from the mercantile elements from which their families originally came. Huppert maintains that society never recognized these "gentry" as a class, that they never fitted into the early modern social schema.

Like Wood and Dewald, I find the traditional interpretation of the French nobility to be simplistic, unsubstantiated, and fundamentally incorrect. And like Schalk, I agree that a shift took place in the meaning of nobility, so that by the middle of the seventeenth century noble status was associated with pedigree. Unlike Huppert, I do not find the anoblis to have lived rigidly separate lives. Rather, I am convinced that tremendous assimilation between old and new occurred during the early modern period, that traditional generalizations about opposing nobilities and an aristocratic crisis are highly misinformed, and that elite society was able to accommodate an infusion from below.

I would add that the old generalizations are also flawed due to their exclusive consideration of the standards of the northern aristocracy, a group whose lives had for centuries revolved around their châteaux and their military duties. Yet as far back as the Roman Empire, the aristocracy of southern France had not followed this pattern, developing instead the custom of living primarily in towns. Seventeenth-century Aix-en-Provence, for example, was home to a large noble population that, although inflated by the presence of anoblis who had purchased offices, also included many old noble

7. George Huppert, *Les Bourgeois Gentilshommes: An Essay on the Definition of Elites in Renaissance France* (Chicago, 1977).

families whose ancestors had lived in town for centuries. From their urban base the nobles of Aix, both old and new, commanded spheres of influence that encompassed provincial politics, royal government, municipal life, and the local economy. Urban location was only one of several ways in which the Aixois and other southern nobles differed from their northern counterparts. The survival of Roman law, the evolution of a unique system of land tenure, and the incomplete development of feudalism also distinguished the Midi and its aristocracy. Such regional diversity was intrinsic to France in the early modern period and inevitably affected the strength of provincial nobilities.

Through analyses of social structure, wealth, marriage, inheritance, education, and civic activity, this work examines the native nobility of Aix during the seventeenth century. Such a study poses some important methodological problems. First, in a town like Aix, seat of sovereign courts, with the local aristocratic population swollen by the presence of nobles who held offices in those courts and lived in Aix at least part of the year, how does one identify a "native nobility"? It is not easily done, and no doubt some Aixois were inadvertently omitted from this study, and other families included who should not have been. My decision to add any particular family was based in part on those official investigations into the authenticity of nobility known as the *recherches,* in part on genealogical materials, and in part on my own intuition about that family—a feeling that, no matter how unscientific, was nevertheless guided by exposure to the sources.[8] After much deliberation, I arrived at a list of eighty-one extended families whose residence in Aix was well established. My criteria for the inclusion of anoblis required long-standing residence in Aix prior to ennoblement. This provision was designed to exclude those who had established themselves in the town only recently, as a consequence of holding office in the royal courts.

The next problem was how to test traditional assumptions about the structure and nature of the nobility, assumptions that I feel rather strongly do not strictly apply to the southern nobility—namely, the notion of a sword-robe conflict. The obvious way would have been to isolate the "sword" families from this group of eighty-one and

8. For an excellent description of the recherches and their significance, see Wood, *Nobility of the Election of Bayeux,* 25–42.

examine their interaction with the remaining, presumably "robe" families. This would have been, in my opinion, impossible. I am convinced that the concept of *robe* is inappropriate for the nobility of Aix, and for much of southern France, for the very same reason that the term *sword* is largely inappropriate: As used by the crisis historians, the two terms are virtually defined through their opposition, the existence of one implying the existence of the other. Yet among the peculiarities of the southern aristocracy is the fact that they were not a by-product of feudalism. An aristocracy of Gallo-Roman stock predated the arrival of vassalage, and through the centuries one could be noble in the south and still remain independent of feudal ties. Southern elites were based on wealth and antiquity, but not on valor. Fiefs and infeudation remained superfluous to nobility in the Midi— although many southern nobles sought their additional prestige— and ennoblement occurred in the Middle Ages without them. Thus the southern elites were never a true "sword" nobility, a point that in itself invalidates the sword-robe construct.

Aix, like other provincial capitals in the sixteenth and seventeenth centuries, was the scene of rapid upward mobility and instantaneous ennoblement through service in the Parlement, the Cour des Comptes, and the généralité (an administrative unit in the royal fiscal system), or through purchase of letters of ennoblement. The effects of this social change on the native nobility were clearly profound. How does one evaluate them, if not in terms of sword and robe? I have chosen to substitute the categories *old* and *new*. Those terms will appear throughout this study, along with *anoblis,* which I use synonymously with *new.* By new, or anoblis, I mean families ennobled after 1500. Certainly, families were ennobled prior to 1500; in one sense all noble families were at some point in their genealogies anoblis. But I refer to a specific phenomenon, that of the families who profited from the venal offices and the letters of nobility associated with the supposed period of aristocratic crisis. Of the eighty-one extended native-noble families in Aix, I classified thirty-eight as old and forty-three as anoblis, or new.

It is very important to note here that other historians writing about Aix have not abandoned the conventional categories in describing aristocratic society. In her study of the eighteenth-century parlementaires of Aix, Monique Cubells continues to rely on the concepts of sword and robe.[9] She insists that the *robins* shared with sword families in the status of nobility, that they enjoyed a parallel rather than an inferior status and existence. Although she acknowledges that there were links between the two groups, she continues to write in terms of robe solidarity and a large measure of separateness and autonomy. As a result, many of her interpretations and conclusions for the seventeenth century differ significantly from my own. For example, in adhering to the sword-robe system of classification in reference to the two groups' respective participation in the Parlement, Cubells indicates very little officeholding by the sword faction. This, however, is easily explained. First, as I have just pointed out, the nobility of Provence, even during the Middle Ages, was never truly or completely chivalric. Second, normal rates of demographic attrition over the centuries reduced the number of families that could legitimately claim to be *chevaleresque* in origin. By the seventeenth and eighteenth centuries, as Cubells herself acknowledges, few so-called sword families were left to enter the Parlement.[10] Does this really imply robe solidarity? What about the families ennobled in the late Middle Ages? Are they really part of Cubells' *robins*? And are they really so distinct from her "sword" families? To repeat, I have chosen to include them in the "old" nobility (which carries the fragments of what might have been a sword) because they are medieval in origin and their nobility is not associated with the period and trends that supposedly created the robe.

All in all, it seems to me that the sword-robe construct is artificial to the historical experience of Aix, and that it therefore renders artificial and flawed results when used as a diagnostic tool. I suggest that it is time for historians of Aix, and perhaps for historians of other provincial nobilities, to put sword and robe behind us and to examine changes in elite society using other means. I am not implying that the sixteenth century did not witness important changes in elite society, in Aix as well as elsewhere, but rather that these changes might be better addressed in new ways. What I have done here is to examine the native nobility of Aix—those eighty-one extended families—comparing those who were nobles before the sixteenth

9. Monique Cubells, *La Provence des Lumières: Les parlementaires d'Aix au XVIIIe siècle* (Paris, 1984).

10. *Ibid.*, 33–34.

century with those who were ennobled as a result of the historical forces of that century and the next.

Although I deal with data pertaining to all eighty-one families, five families—two old and three new—are profiled throughout. That number is small enough to provide a sense of continuity and family strategy, particularly with regard to marriage and inheritance. It would have been possible to increase my sample of testaments and marriage contracts, but only at the expense of this continuity. Family strategies and ambitions become fully recognizable only in the context of the affairs of all siblings over generations, and larger numbers and a statistically more reliable sample would have made it awkward, if not impossible, to sort out all the relationships among wealth, status, size of families, political influence, clientage, legal rights, and family honor.

An unfortunate effect of this methodological choice is that it sacrifices hierarchy for the analytic concept of class or group. In one of the brilliant sets of remarks that one has come to expect of him, Professor Orest Ranum laments the fact that social historians, who usually peer at the seventeenth century through the diachronic tunnel, have flattened out groups, so that signs of hierarchy are generally absent from their studies.[11] So it is with this study. But I think the sacrifice is necessary if one is to examine social phenomena such as assimilation. Two groups must be identified separately and examined collectively, and in the process traditional nomenclatures are obscured.

Finally, why Aix-en-Provence? Some would argue that the very characteristics that attracted me to Aix as the subject for a local study also make it an unreliable example from which to generalize about the larger French nobility. My purpose is not, however, to offer new generalizations about the French nobility; rather, it is to suggest that there are some notable exceptions to long-established generalizations. Aix and its native nobility were truly exceptional. Visitors in the seventeenth century remarked on this, just as modern visitors recognize the essentially Mediterranean character of the town, a character that is easily perceived in the lyrical accent that persists and in the rhythm of life. In her study of judicial politics and revolt,

11. Orest Ranum, "Comment on Session: Social and Urban Aspects of the Grand Siècle," in *Proceedings of the Western Society for French History,* XI (1984), 61–63.

Sharon Kettering vividly describes the very complex political life of the town.[12] She writes about factional intrigues, political opportunism, and Provençal recalcitrance as causal forces in the political disturbances and violence that were recurrent features of municipal life in the early seventeenth century. Cissie Fairchilds, in her study of the changing nature of charity, provides a different and complementary view of Aix, that of the *ville hospitalière,* the "charitable town"— a view that is essentially from the bottom looking up.[13]

Although they have studied Aix from vastly different perspectives and for entirely different reasons, both Kettering and Fairchilds acknowledge its administrative and aristocratic character. The wealthy and the privileged, the noblesse, were an overwhelming presence in the early modern town, and indeed still are. One is reminded of them by their architectural remains, the abundant townhouses (*hôtels*) whose Italianate facades and substantial masonry constitute the dominant architectural element of the *centre de ville*. Historians of architecture have long appreciated these structures and their concentration in Aix, both for their essential aesthetic qualities and as representations of a very specific society and culture. Such features are modern vestiges of the historically unique society and culture of southern France, which together created a nobility that diverged in crucial ways from the model of the northern aristocracy. And it is precisely for this divergence that the native nobility of Aix deserves attention in the current historical debate.

12. Sharon Kettering, *Judicial Politics and Urban Revolt in Seventeenth-Century France: The Parlement of Aix, 1629–1659* (Princeton, 1978).
13. Cissie C. Fairchilds, *Poverty and Charity in Aix-en-Provence, 1640–1789* (Baltimore, 1976).

I

URBANISM AND NOBILITY
IN THE MIDI

From Roman times through the early modern period, the custom of nobles living in towns distinguished the Midi from northern France. Over the centuries southern nobles tended to concentrate in urban areas, establishing a social and residential pattern unique to the region. Long before the arrival of sovereign courts in the sixteenth century (an event that necessarily increased the aristocratic element in any town's population), Aix-en-Provence was the primary residence of large numbers of nobles, who controlled municipal institutions, dominated town life, and played a vital role in provincial politics. Their urban residency was only one of several ways in which the Aixois and other southern nobles differed from their northern counterparts; the continued use of Roman law, the survival of large tracts of allodial (nonfeudal) property, and the imperfect development of vassalage also set the Midi and its elites apart from the remainder of the kingdom. Yet of all the traits that marked the southern nobility, the most striking was their tendency to locate in old Roman towns such as Aix. That so many southern nobles chose to remain in towns rather than reside on country estates stemmed originally from the Roman legacy to the Mediterranean region. The Roman Empire, with an urban power center at its heart, introduced city dwelling to tribal peoples as a means of controlling and civilizing them.[1]

· After the empire's decline, many Mediterranean areas continued

1. Lewis Mumford, *The City in History* (New York, 1961), 205.

to follow the Roman way of life, a course still possible because not all towns and cities perished during the widespread turmoil that accompanied the fall of Rome. In fact, this urban tradition enabled inhabitants of southern Europe to rely on their cities for security and defense against invaders, and the military function of towns and cities in turn contributed to their preservation. Similarly, through the continued use of towns and cities as ecclesiastical centers, bishops and other churchmen also played a role in their survival.[2]

Well before the high Middle Ages, fundamental differences between northern and southern patterns of settlement had become quite firmly established. Edith Ennen has identified three distinct zones of residency that evolved out of the varying impact that Roman civilization and the barbarian invasions had on Europe. The first zone includes Germany north and east of the Rhine, and Scandinavia—areas that experienced no direct influence from Rome and thus no urban development. The second zone consists of northern France and the Danubian region; Mediterranean culture, including some urban development, successfully penetrated this area during the period of the Roman Empire, but the Germanic invasions almost completely eliminated any vestige of the Roman presence. The Mediterranean area itself, including southern France, forms the third zone. Here the old urban culture continued to exist after Rome's decline, and towns still provided the characteristic habitat.[3]

Having experienced more urban development and suffered less destruction from the invasions than its northern counterpart, Mediterranean society was able to preserve its Roman urban tradition. Even with the revival of commerce and growth of northern towns in the eleventh and twelfth centuries, northern and southern Europe continued to evolve differently simply because the south had never reverted to an entirely rural state. The Mediterranean regions re-

2. Michael I. Rostovtzeff, *A History of the Ancient World,* trans. J. D. Duff (2 vols.; 1927; rpr. New York, 1945), I, 243; Edith Ennen, *The Medieval Town,* trans. Natalie Fryde (New York, 1979), 20; Georges Duby, "Les Villes du sud-est de la Gaule du VIIIe au XIe siècles," in *Hommes et structures du Moyen-Age,* ed. Georges Duby (Paris, 1973), 114; Janet Roebuck, *The Shaping of Urban Society: A History of City Forms and Functions* (New York, 1974), 39.

3. Edith Ennen, "The Different Types of Formation of European Towns," in *Early Medieval Society,* ed. Sylvia Thrupp (New York, 1967), 175.

mained more mature, more densely populated, and more urban than the north.[4]

Within the context of Roman heritage and urban development, an aristocracy arose in southern France that was in many ways unique. The aristocracy of northern France developed from military necessity along traditional feudal lines, but in the south of France an aristocracy of Gallo-Roman stock predated the appearance of feudalism in the region. Their positions as great allodial proprietors and their relation to the old senatorial class of the empire enabled this wealthy elite to emerge as an aristocracy prior to the arrival of vassalage. Jean-Pierre Poly and Eric Bournazel claim that as late as the eleventh century, the aristocracy of Provence still clung to the fact of their Roman ancestry.[5]

Land was one of the original bases for the southern aristocracy, and land tenure in the region differed from the way in which land was held elsewhere, particularly in the widespread existence of allodial property. An *allod* was land that involved no recognition of overlordship; the owner of an allod could sell or give it away at will because possession was free from service, rent, and homage and fealty. Legal scholars maintain that it was the survival of Roman law in most parts of the south that ensured the preservation of allodial rights. The allod was certainly most common in those areas of southern France that fell under the jurisdiction of written law rather than custom. Roman law upheld the allodial regime because it affirmed the rights of the individual and recognized the power of the written contract, thereby opposing feudal subordination in favor of the absolute power of the individual proprietor over his property.[6]

The somewhat tardy introduction of feudalism to the Midi meant, of course, that the proportion of allodial property began to decrease

4. Gérard Sautel, "Les Villes du Midi méditerranéen au Moyen-Age: Aspects économiques et sociaux, IXe–XIIIe siècles," in *Recueils de la Société Jean Bodin,* VII, Pt. 2 (1955), 321; John Mundy and Peter Reisenburg, *The Medieval Town* (Princeton, 1958), 94.

5. Patrick J. Geary, *Aristocracy in Provence: The Rhône Basin at the Dawn of the Carolingian Age* (Philadelphia, 1985), 105–106; Jean-Pierre Poly and Eric Bournazel, *La Mutation féodale* (Paris, 1980), 315–35.

6. Eleanor Lodge, *Gascony Under English Rule* (London, 1926), 194–96; D. Brissaud, *Les Anglais en Guyenne* (Paris, 1875), 18–19; Pierre Belperron, *La Croisade contre les Albigeois et l'union de Languedoc à la France, 1209–1249* (Paris, 1942), 18–19.

relative to the growing numbers of fiefs. But the allod remained quite important in the region through the early modern period, and as recently as the seventeenth century the proportion of property held in fief in Provence was rather low when compared with the amount of property that was still allodial.[7] This situation clearly reflects the lasting influence of Roman law and the difficulties presented vassalage in the region.

Just as the presence of the allod distinguished land tenure in the Midi, it also influenced the character of the southern aristocracy. During the Middle Ages allodial property and Roman law frequently obstructed and almost always complicated infeudation in the south, so that many nobles never owned a fief and never owed an overlord service or homage. Having evolved in northern France during the period of the Viking invasions and under the influence of various Germanic institutions, feudalism was essentially a northern phenomenon. In its subsequent introduction to the south of France, the system of vassalage naturally was adapted to southern circumstances; as a result, it assumed a significantly altered form. Feudalism in the south merely reaffirmed the existing social hierarchy, one whose upper class might be more accurately described as a wealthy *noblesse de race*.[8] The medieval knights of southern France were often descended from the same older ruling families that had dominated the region for generations. After the arrival of vassalage, the manner in which these families exercised power simply changed or expanded. Whereas the upper class had previously wielded power as rich allodial proprietors, they did so now as knights or *milites* as well, so that aristocratic society became a cousinship of nobles and knights attempting to maintain both economic and political power. Overall, the introduction of vassalage did not change the basic social structure of the south, but rather was grafted haphazardly onto that structure.[9]

7. E. Duprat, "Le Haut Moyen-Age," in *BDR,* II, 266; René Pillorget, *Les Mouvements insurrectionnels de Provence entre 1596 et 1715* (Paris, 1975), 82.

8. Georges Duby, "Lineage, Nobility, and Chivalry in the Region of Mâcon During the Twelfth Century," in *Family Society: Selections from the "Annales: économies, sociétés, civilisations,"* ed. Robert Forster and Orest Ranum (Baltimore, 1976), 36–40.

9. Archibald R. Lewis, *The Development of Southern French and Catalan Society, 719–1050* (Austin, 1965), 287, 313; Duby, "Lineage, Nobility, and Chivalry," 36–40; Georges Duby, *La Société au XIe et XIIe siècles dans la région mâconnaise* (Paris, 1971), 151.

Because of a dearth of records for this early period, historians cannot explain why or how vassalage was introduced to the Midi. Nor have their efforts to describe its early development been particularly successful. What they have succeeded in doing is describing at length the peculiarities of the southern feudal structure, which was weaker and more loosely organized than that of northern France.[10] Although the ideal feudal pyramid never existed, one could argue that the northern aristocracy did achieve a considerable degree of rank and subordination among its members. But in the Midi, feudal ties between allodial proprietors of equal wealth often made it impossible to force compliance with the obligations of vassalage, and particularly within the upper ranks of the nobility, vassals ignored responsibilities to their overlords. Feudal ties appear to have been strong only when they bound a powerful overlord and a lesser noble who, not owning large tracts of allodial property, truly depended on his fief for subsistence.[11]

Yet in spite of the fact that feudal obligations were frequently neglected, many southern nobles chose to enter these relationships. Georges Duby explains southern infeudation as a reflection of the natural combativeness characteristic of aristocracy; that is, he suggests that knighthood provided the old southern aristocracy with a more precise class definition through an ethos that focused on a profession of arms and judicial privileges. Robert Boutruche, however, writes that in Bordelais during the Hundred Years' War, knighthood became a luxury affordable only to very powerful nobles. As a result, the nobility there evolved as a clear hierarchy of "les barons, les chevaliers, les écuyers, et les gentils."[12] In contrast with northern France, in the Midi one might be noble without being a knight, and many southern nobles remained independent of the system of vassalage during the Middle Ages.

With these distinguishing traits of an urban tradition and a unique aristocracy, southern society never produced the sharp distinctions between burgher and knight, town and country, that were typical of the more feudal northern provinces. Instead, the social composition

10. Henri Sée, *Les Classes rurales et la régime domanial en France au Moyen-Age* (Paris, 1901), 137.

11. Duby, *La Société . . . mâconnaise,* 159–64.

12. *Ibid;* Robert Boutruche, *La Crise d'une société: Seigneurs et paysans du Bordelais pendant la Guerre de Cent Ans* (Paris, 1947), 84.

of most medieval southern towns was a comparatively harmonious mixture of nobles, bourgeois, and the lower classes. The urban nobilities of the Midi, through military and political service, established a civic quality that further distinguished them: they used the towns of the Midi as strategic fortifications against the Moslems, in the process making urban ramparts the basis of protection for the southern populations. As noted earlier, the walled city remained the focus of military life in the south while the castle became the standard fortification elsewhere.[13] In Provence "les chevaliers urbains" were descended from those individuals, endowed with land or some source of wealth, to whom both lay and ecclesiastical authorities had entrusted the defense of the town, and in some instances these nobles actually held their urban dwellings as fiefs in return for service de garde.[14]

In addition to defending towns, southern nobles regarded municipal administration as their duty, if not their preserve—an attitude that may have derived from the old Roman tradition of service to the state. By the high Middle Ages, councils were the governing authorities of most southern towns, and local aristocrats were quick to assume control of these bodies. Membership in the earliest councils in Languedoc came exclusively from the nobility; only later did the bourgeoisie join. In most medieval southern towns, however, nobles shared responsibilities with wealthy merchants, forming a type of ruling oligarchy or patriciate similar to the *grandi* of Italian towns, and they joined town life more as members of the community than as seigneurs. Nobles mixed freely with the bourgeoisie; they married with it on occasion; they pursued some of the same commercial ventures; and they shared municipal offices with it, albeit usually with an uneven division of power.[15]

13. Sautel, "Les Villes du Midi," 337; Mundy and Reisenburg, *Medieval Town*, 48, Marc Bloch, *Feudal Society,* trans. L. A. Manyon (Chicago, 1961), 299; Duby, "Les Villes du Sud-Est," 113–114, 126.

14. Edouard Baratier, "Marquisats et comtés en Provence," in *Histoire de la Provence*, ed. Edouard Baratier (Toulouse, 1969), 146–47; Sautel, "Les Villes du Midi," 337.

15. Mundy and Riesenburg, *Medieval Town,* 45; Philippe Wolfe, *Histoire du Languedoc* (Toulouse, 1967), 159–60; A. Dupont, "L'Evolution sociale du consulat nîmois du milieu du XIIIe au milieu du XVIe siècle," in *Annales du Midi,* LXXII (1960),

By the sixteenth century this association of noble and bourgeois was not limited to the towns of the Midi. As the French monarchy, a victim of inflation and the rising costs of dynastic rivalries, sought additional means of financing its indebtedness, it created avenues for upward mobility and ennoblement. The sale of *lettres d'anoblissement* and the venality of office sponsored by the monarchy enabled the more successful and socially ambitious members of the bourgeoisie to become anoblis. As this process of upward mobility took place in towns that, like Aix, had numerous opportunities and offices to offer, it inevitably affected the local social composition. Provincial capitals in northern France also experienced these social changes, but even though some officeholding nobles in the north resided in the towns where sovereign courts were located, the older, traditional noble families generally remained on their estates, and gradually the so-called robe nobility joined them there. These anoblis, eager for acceptance and approval by those whose lives they emulated, also purchased estates and if possible used them as their primary residences. In the élection of Bayeux, for example, most anoblis followed the example of the rural squirearchy by settling in the countryside.[16] In sum, although the wholesale ennoblements of the sixteenth century profoundly affected the nobility by the infusion of new blood and new money, they did not permanently eliminate one of the fundamental distinctions between the northern nobles and the aristocracy of the Midi. The lives of the nothern nobility, both old and new, continued to revolve around their country estates; the southerners continued to make their homes in town.

The Midi, of course, was not without châteaux. If financially able, southern nobles usually owned both an hôtel and a château. But most families regarded the hôtel as their primary residence, and for some it was their sole residence. The many unoccupied châteaux in Provence and the Midi, often in a state of disrepair, testified to the preeminence of the townhouse and the urban way of life. The ennoblements of the sixteenth century did not change the southern

---

289–90; *BDR*, II, 690; Baratier, "Marquisats et comtés," 146–47; Maurice Agulhon, *La Vie sociale en Provence intérieure au lendemain de la Révolution,* in *Bibliothèque d'histoire révolutionnaire,* Sér. 3, No. 12 (1970), 90.

16. Wood, *Nobility of the Election of Bayeux,* 80–81.

preference for town living; rather, the anoblis simply joined the ranks of the urban elite. By 1600 Aix was no longer merely a typical southern town with a healthy nobility; instead, it had become a virtual enclave of nobles, truly a *ville aristocratique*.[17]

Originally named Aquae Sextius because of the nearby thermal waters, Aix was founded by Calvinus Sextius in the 120s B.C. as the first Roman post in transalpine Gaul. It became the political capital and seat of the provincial governor, and remarkably, its growth continued almost unaffected by the fall of the empire. With the succession of the Christian emperors and the arrival of its first bishop in 375, Aix became the religious center of the southern Roman provinces as well. During the Middle Ages the counts of Provence held their courts at Aix, and until the succession of the House of Anjou it remained the political capital. The Angevin counts divided their time between Aix and Angers until 1471, when "le bon roi René" chose to return permanently to Aix, a decision historians regard as the beginning of a renaissance that lasted until the Revolution.[18]

Contributing to that renaissance was the union of Provence with the royal domain in the late fifteenth century and the subsequent arrivals in Aix of the Parlement (1501) and the Cour des Comptes (1555). The presence of royal government and sovereign courts stimulated population growth: at a time when much of Europe suffered recurring demographic and subsistence crises, the population of Aix increased from around 22,000 or 23,000 in 1627 to over 27,000 in 1695.[19] Opportunities for advancement offered by the courts attracted ambitious outsiders whose arrivals in town heightened an increasingly bureaucratic atmosphere. Traditional (or "sword") nobles, administrative (or "robe") nobles, and a very important group with characteristics of both all congregated in Aix. They participated in municipal and royal government, dominated the surrounding countryside, and lived on the rents and revenues of scattered properties, judicial offices, and various other investments. At the same time they

17. Agulhon, *La Vie sociale en Provence,* 90–91; A. Bourde, "La Provence baroque, 1596–1660," in *Histoire de la Provence,* ed. Edouard Baratier (Toulouse, 1969), 280.

18. Paul-Albert Février, "Antiquité et haut Moyen-Age: Les Débuts d'une cité," in *Histoire d'Aix-en-Provence* (Paris, 1977), 27–57, *passim;* Noel Coulet, "Naissance et épanouissement d'une capitale: Aix au Moyen-Age," *ibid.,* 68–109, *passim.*

19. Coulet, "Naissance et épanouissement d'une capitale," 68–109; Kettering, *Judicial Politics,* 23.

figured prominently in expansive networks of alliances with the entire Provençal nobility, and by this means they extended their influence throughout the province and beyond.

Aristocratic interests, both old and new, fostered a complex social and political milieu—a noble environment carefully documented at the end of the seventeenth century. In 1695 the royal government ordered a survey of the human resources of the realm, or all "les bouches qui mangent du pain." Lebret, the intendant for Provence, conducted a rigorous accounting of all the communities within his jurisdiction. He directed his staff to proceed house by house, carefully recording the names and occupations of all heads of household and the number and sex of their dependents. The survey also included the households of widows and the inhabitants of religious houses and charitable institutions.[20] By its thoroughness and detail, the resulting *registre de capitation* has given historians a remarkably complete set of demographic data. In 1970 Jean Paul Coste collated the material pertaining to Aix to reveal more about the residential and occupational aspects of its inhabitants.[21]

In 1695 Aix had a total population of 27,512 inhabitants distributed among 11,201 separate households (*ménages*). Coste's figures establish the remarkable fact that the combined nobility ac-

20. Jacqueline Carrière, *La Population d'Aix-en-Provence à la fin du XVIIe siècle: Etude de démographie historique d'après le registre de capitation de 1695* (Aix, 1958), 12–15.

21. See Jean Paul Coste, *La Ville d'Aix en 1695: Structure urbaine et société* (2 vols.; Aix, 1970), II, 749–816, *passim*. It is important to note that although the figures in this chapter and Appendix I are based on information taken from Coste's work, they are not the same as those listed in Coste's summary tables. Coste includes certain nonnoble professionals and officeholders as nobles in table C (p. 712) because they do not fit into his professional schema elsewhere. Specifically, he designates occupations such as *huissiers*, *greffiers*, and *notaires* as part of the "petite robe." Since I am interested in nobles exclusively, I eliminate such individuals from my figures, which accounts for the discrepancies between our tables.

Coste established a set of criteria to use in separating nobles from commoners. A title, of course, was the most reliable way of recognizing a noble. References to fiefs might also indicate nobility, although alone they could not guarantee it, since some commoners owned fiefs. Often a qualifying term, *écuyer,* would follow the name of a noble, and less frequently the word *noble* itself appeared in the register to signify "écuyer." Finally, military commissions or functions could identify nobles, particularly membership in the order of the Knights of Malta. Beyond these criteria, Coste also relied on genealogical information and on his own knowledge of the Provençal nobility to classify a particular household as noble or *roturier*.

counted for 12.75 percent of this population. As Fairchilds writes, "Aix was a focal point for the various overlapping webs which characterized bureaucratic organization under the Old Regime." Its nobility was a diverse group (see Appendix I) that included old noble families whose presence stemmed from tradition and anoblis who had profited from opportunities in the royal bureaucracy. By 1695 Aix had become a town of the wealthy and the poor and very little else. Entrepreneurial elements accounted for only 9.1 percent of the population and were sandwiched between the nobility and those who served the nobility.[22]

The figures for nobles in Aix contrast rather dramatically with those for the northern town of Amiens. Very few noble families resided in Amiens during the seventeenth and eighteenth centuries. Pierre Deyon notes that although nobles came into town for "les réceptions princières et les processions," they rarely chose to make Amiens their principal residence. Using the roll of the *ban* and *arrière-ban*—that is, the list of names of individuals who responded to the royal muster called in times of emergency—Deyon was able to determine the number of noble households in Amiens for 1675. He discovered that only 21 households of traditional nobles existed in Amiens that year, constituting only .32 percent of the total households. In 1698 the intendant recorded 500 noble families in his généralité, 86 of which belonged to the élection of Amiens. Pierre Goubert records similar patterns for Beauvais. In 1696 only 4 out of 3,660 households in the city of Beauvais belonged to the traditional nobility.[23]

Coste's data incorporated noble families who were not native to Aix, living there only part of the year because of the sovereign courts. But it is the native Aixois, both old nobles and new, who form the subject matter of the remaining chapters, for in their heritage of urban dwelling they preserved one of the main characteristics that distinguished the southern aristocracy and the Midi, and their activities and way of life necessarily varied from those of the northern counterparts.

22. *Ibid.;* Fairchilds, *Poverty and Charity in Aix,* 5, 9–10.
23. Pierre Deyon, *Amiens, capitale provinciale: Etude sur la société urbaine au XVIIe siècle* (Paris, 1967), 266; Pierre Goubert, *The Ancien Régime: French Society, 1600–1750,* trans. Steve Cox (2 vols.; New York, 1969), I, 224–25.

II

STRUCTURE AND WEALTH

The fact of urban residence not only distinguished the native nobility of Aix from provincial nobilities in northern France, but it also shaped the structure, nature, and society of the Aixois elite in ways that raise serious questions about one of the main components of the crisis interpretation, the sword-robe construct. The city of Aix provided an environment in which assimilation between old and new families was not only possible, it was inevitable. (This is not to imply that assimilation was impossible elsewhere in France; certainly, Wood and Dewald have confirmed its occurrence among nobles in Bayeux and Rouen, and those findings, too, seriously challenge the traditional notion of sword-robe conflict.)[1] As a result of the considerable integration between old and new in Aix, the social structure was far more fluid than the rigid sword-robe division traditionally described by historians. Families often differed in antiquity and wealth, but rarely in occupations or functions. The city offered a variety of sources of income and investment—particularly the opportunity to purchase office—to old and new families alike, a fact that played a crucial role in preventing the traditionally proclaimed separation.

The urban nature of the Aixois nobility creates problems of classification for the historian. The old sword-robe nomenclature is not appropriate, for although the term *robe* has some application in a city that was the seat of provincial government, *sword* is of much more limited usefulness. The old native families of Aix were not really sword nobles, not really a warrior aristocracy. Certainly, they owned

1. Wood, *Nobility of the Election of Bayeux;* Dewald, *Formation of a Provincial Nobility.*

21

fiefs and exhibited related *marques de noblesse,* but many could not claim chivalric origins. Some families' claims to nobility were immemorial, extending back to the Gallo-Roman aristocracy. Many other families, however, were anoblis of the fourteenth and fifteenth centuries—a period of significant upward mobility in Provence and elsewhere (and one that needs more study by social historians).[2] They typically had started as attorneys, notaries, or merchants in medieval Provence and had attained noble status before 1500. These anoblis from the period of the Angevin counts have been included with the old nobility because their claims to nobility predate the arrival of sovereign courts, the venality of office, and the period of wholesale social ascendancy that created the famous noblesse de robe so familiar to us now. Regardless of origins, early or late medieval, their orientation was urban, administrative, and occasionally mercantile, and had been for centuries, which necessarily made these old families something other than a sword nobility. To reiterate a point I made in the Introduction, the sword-robe construct is not applicable to Aix, and to much of southern France, because the concept of sword is not. Without a sword, there cannot be a robe, for the latter is defined in terms of a hostile relationship to the former.[3]

In 1695 the noble population of Aix included a total of 596 households, 196 of which belonged to men who held offices in the courts (see Appendix I).[4] It is impossible to classify all of these 196 households as a separate and distinct robe nobility because nearly half of them exhibit traditional marques de noblesse such as owning fiefs, and 20 of that fraction held the title of count, marquis, or baron. Of course, it was common for anoblis to acquire fiefs; it was also common for old noble families in Aix to invest in the courts. These numerous fiefholding magistrates, especially the 20 titled ones, merely confirm that the nobility of Aix lends itself to neither description nor analysis in the conventional categories.

Using genealogical materials and, more important, the 1667 recherche into authenticity of nobility, it is possible to establish not only the number of old families whose members served in the courts,

2. Edouard Perroy acknowledges the extent and importance of this social mobility of the late Middle Ages. See Perroy, "Social Mobility Among the French *Noblesse* in the Later Middle Ages," *Past and Present,* XXI (1962), 25–38.

3. Mousnier, *Institutions of France,* I, 159–65.

4. Coste, *La Ville d'Aix en 1695,* II, 749–816, *passim.*

but also the number of recently ennobled families that were Aixois.[5] The purpose of the recherches was to detect usurpers and "return them to the tax rolls." Families presented to the commission documentary evidence of their nobility—genealogies, marriage contracts, testaments, letters patent for offices, *arrêts* of the sovereign courts, certification of military service, and in the cases of many recently ennobled families, letters of ennoblement. In 1667 a family that could prove nobility before 1560 was certified of ancient lineage. According to Wood, the recherches had the important effects of regulating the membership and reinforcing the juridical status of nobility.[6]

With information from the 1667 recherche, I identified 81 extended families as members of the local nobility—that is, as native Aixois nobles. Further, I was able to classify 38 of those families as old nobles and 43 as new. (Again, I defined a family as old if its claims to nobility were well established by 1500, the year before the arrival of the Parlement in Aix, with the subsequent period of widespread social advancement through the purchase of judicial and financial offices.) Of these 81 native noble families, 67 held at least one office in government during the century, including offices in the Parlement, the Cour des Comptes, the *sénéchaussée* (a judicial unit intermediate in level between the Parlement and the seigneurial courts), and the généralité.[7] Unlike what one would expect from the traditional sword-robe viewpoint, new nobles did not dominate the officeholding. In fact, old and new families held offices in almost equal proportion (see table 1).

Clearly, royal government in Aix was not strictly the preserve of anoblis. On the contrary, many members of cadet and lesser branches of old and venerable houses regularly bought positions in the courts, and very often members of the main branches of these families joined

5. The list of noble families was compiled from material included in the following sources: B. Méjanes MS 1133, "Jugement de la noblesse de Provence, 1667;" B. Méjanes MS 1134, "Répertoire des jugements de noblesse rendus par les commissaires députés par Sa Majesté, en l'année 1667. . . ."; Artefeuil [pseud.], *Histoire héroïque et universelle de la noblesse de Provence* (2 vols.; Avignon, 1757); François-Paul Blanc, *Origines des familles provençales maintenues dans le second ordre sous le règne de Louis XIV: Dictionnaire généalogique* (Aix, Thèse de droit, 1971).

6. Wood, *Nobility of the Election of Bayeux*, 25, 29–30, 42.

7. Material on all officeholding families is found in Balthasar de Clapiers-Collongues, *Chronologie des officiers des cours souveraines, publiée, annotée, et augmentée par le marquis de Boisgelin* (Aix, 1909–12).

TABLE 1

Offices Held by Old and New Noble Families

	Held Offices	Held No Offices	Totals
Old Families	31	7	38
New Families	36	7	43
Totals	67	14	81

Source: Balthasar de Clapiers-Collongues, *Chronologie des officiers des cours souveraines, publiée, annotée, et augmentée par le marquis de Boisgelin* (Aix, 1909–12).

them in senior positions. One such family was the Forbins, who while commanding an impressive collection of titles, fiefs, and other properties throughout the region could also boast two first presidents, three presidents *à mortier,* and several councillors in the Parlement during the seventeenth century.[8] The mere fact that nearly half of the officeholding families of Aix were older families like the Forbins should be sufficient to raise a question about the usefulness of the sword-robe construct.

That the local nobility included forty-three families of more recent origin suggests that Aix had been the scene of large-scale ennoblement. This process in some instances took place as the result of service to the king or occupation of specific offices, but most anoblis purchased lettres d'anoblissement. Kettering discovered that 48 percent of the men serving in the Parlement of Aix during the period 1629 to 1649 came from families ennobled in the sixteenth century, most by letters.[9] Ennoblement by letter continued to take place in Provence at a remarkably constant rate through the first half of the seventeenth century, as François-Paul Blanc has shown in his study of the origins of the larger Provençal nobility as well as the rates for ennoblement in the region during the reigns of Henry III and his Bourbon successors (see table 2). The slight increase in letters under Louis XIV is misleading; his search for faux nobles during the recherches meant that many families sought and subsequently received *lettres de confirmation de lettres revoqués.*

8. *Ibid.*

9. Jeanne Allemand, *La haute société aixoise dans la second moitié du XVIIIe siècle* (Aix, Thèse de droit, 1927), 21–23; Kettering, *Judicial Politics,* 216.

TABLE 2

Ennoblement by Letters in Provence

Reign	Number of Families Ennobled	Average Per Year
Henry III (1574–1589)	11	.73
Henry IV (1589–1610)	15	.71
Louis XIII (1610–1643)	24	.73
Louis XIV (1643–1715)	71	.99

Source: François-Paul Blanc, "L'anoblissement par lettres en Provence à l'époque des réformations de Louis XIV" (Aix, Thèse de droit, 1971).

The recherches were critical events in the history of the Provençal aristocracy because until the reign of Louis XIV usurpations of noble status had occurred rather frequently in the region. Before 1500 the entire Provençal aristocracy consisted of only 108 separate families and their various branches. Genealogists estimate that 33 of these families were descended from very old aristocratic lines dating from the early Middle Ages and that 54 others had received letters of nobility or authorization to infeudate (which under the Angevin counts had the same result as letter ennoblement). The state of affairs changed dramatically between 1550 and 1673, a period of wholesale ennoblement during which 220 new families joined the aristocracy; of these, 134 were ennobled legally by letter and 86 usurped their status by various means.[10]

One of the most common methods of usurpation was the acquisition of a fief, which in spite of its declining military importance remained a coveted marque de noblesse. Exactly half of the 86 families that usurped nobility between 1550 and 1673 owned fiefs. Although it was quite possible to be ennobled without a fief, possession of any land, whether fief or allod, made upward mobility more likely in this province where tradition was summed up in the saying "Nul seigneur sans terre." Moreover, the peculiar nature of the *taille* in southern France gave fiefs a special significance there. Officials in northern France levied this tax essentially on persons—excluding, of course, members of the aristocracy, the clergy, and the burghers of certain towns. But in the Midi the *taille réelle* fell on nonfeudal land rather

10. Monique Cubells, "A propos des usurpations de noblesse en Provence sous l'Ancien Régime," *Provence historique,* LXXXII (1970), 249, 251–52.

than on people, and a southern noble who owned allodial property would have paid the taille for that property while being exempt from taxes on his fiefs.[11]

The fief was therefore the only way in which to acquire one of the most highly valued privileges of nobility—tax-exempt status—as well as the right to attend assemblies of the provincial estates. Although the proportion of Provençal land held in fief remained low when compared with northern provinces, the number of fiefs in Provence did increase significantly in the sixteenth and seventeenth centuries. To acquire the advantages of fiefholding and to assist themselves in usurping nobility, many families infeudated, some by submitting their land to a suzerain who in turn granted it back as an *arrière-fief*.[12]

Ownership of a fief was perhaps the most important step that a Provençal family could take in usurping noble status, but there were others. Judicial and military careers always tended to reinforce a family's claim to nobility—soldiering for obvious reasons, but law because it had become a new marque de noblesse, and a particularly well-regarded one in this province where legal traditions had been shaped by Roman law. Naturally, any attempt to usurp nobility succeeded only if the family had the requisite wealth. Until the reign of Louis XIV, their various acquisitions and money in general permitted many bourgeois in Provence, as elsewhere, to assume the rank and status of nobility even without its legal recognition, simply because society often came to regard families who could afford to live and conduct themselves like nobles to *be* nobles. To live like nobility was a sign not only of social ambitions, but often of success itself. But Louis XIV's recherches undermined the ennobling power of society, and his vision of absolutism meant that many Provençal families whose claims to nobility had not been legally recognized were condemned as usurpers or faux nobles.[13]

For those anoblis who survived the recherches with nobility intact, fiefs had indeed been crucial investments. The privileges that

11. Schalk, *From Valor to Pedigree*, 155–56; Cubells, "A propos des usurpations," 251–52; Michel Vovelle, "Apogée ou déclin d'une capitale provinciale: Le XVIIIe siècle," in *Histoire d'Aix-en-Provence* (Paris, 1977), 193; Goubert, *Ancien Régime*, I, 165.

12. Allemand, *La haute société aixoise*, 34–36.

13. Schalk, *From Valor to Pedigree*, 159–61; Cubells, "A propos des usurpations," 300.

TABLE 3

Revenue from Fiefs in 1668

	Old Families	New Families
Families assessed	27	25
Fiefs assessed	97	37
Average revenue per family*	4,767	1,280
Average revenue per fief*	1,326	865
Total revenue	128,698	32,008

*In livres-tournois
Source: B. Méjanes, MS 1143 (630-R.732), "Etat du florinage . . . 1668."

fiefholding had long entailed in Provence grew even more attractive in the late sixteenth and the seventeenth centuries. In Aix, only nine of the forty-three newly ennobled native families failed to pattern themselves after the old nobility by acquiring fiefs (all thirty-eight of the old noble families were fiefholders).[14]

How much wealth did the Aixois earn from their fiefs? There is no precise information on feudal revenue for the seventeenth century, but it is possible to form an impression based on the 1668 *af-florinement,* an assessment for a tax levied on fiefs by the Assembly of the Nobility of Provence. In theory the tax was a contribution by the nobility to assist the province in paying soldiers and in funding other expenses. Calculated in florins—hence the name—it was set at one-tenth the value of the revenues from the fief.[15] Not all of the fiefhold-ing Aixois families were listed in the afflorinement, in part because some of the anoblis did not acquire fiefs until after 1668, but the records for those who were assessed reveal a substantial disparity be-tween the holdings of old and new families (see table 3).

14. B. Méjanes, MS 1143 (630-R.732), "Etat du florinage, contenant le revenu noble de tous les fiefs et arrière-fiefs de la province, avec les noms des possesseurs, fait par M. le Premier Président d'Oppède en 1668"; MS 1144, "Afflorinement des biens nobles possedez par les seigneurs feudataires de Provence."

15. B. Méjanes, MS 1143 (630-R.732), "Etat du florinage." A florin was an old monetary unit that corresponded to 60 livres-tournois. As explained by Blanc, 600 livres in revenue would result in a tax of one florin. For an excellent discussion of the afflorinement, see François-Paul Blanc, "L'anoblissement par lettres en Provence à l'époque des reformations de Louis XIV, 1630–1730," *Annales de la Faculté de Droit et de Science Politique d'Aix-Marseille,* LVIII (1972), 677–78. See also BDR, III, 512; Cubells, *La Provence des Lumières,* 83–84.

Not only did the old houses own many more fiefs than the anoblis, but the average value—and undoubtedly the size—of the fiefs owned by old families was also greater. Obviously, old families derived much more wealth from land, certainly from land held in fief, than did new families, a difference reflecting the fact that new families tended to buy a minimal amount of feudal property merely so they could share in the privileges afforded fiefholders. The latter point stands out even more clearly when the revenues from feudal properties as recorded in the afflorinement are listed by individual family (see Appendix IV); besides the families who had no fiefs, many had holdings of relatively little value. It is evident that most of the wealth of anoblis was invested elsewhere—in offices, in urban properties, in allodial holdings, in the loan-investments known as *rentes,* and perhaps still in commerce. Cubells found that this group's investment patterns had changed significantly by the eighteenth century, when the parlementaires put a much greater portion of their total wealth in land, both feudal and allodial, than in any other form of investment.[16] This was clearly not the case in the seventeenth century, when although most new families (thirty-three of forty-three, or 77 percent) did invest in fiefs, they did so on an extremely limited scale. Still, through the acquisition of a fief, even a small fief, they were able to claim some immunity from the taille. At the same time, of course, they became subject to the afflorinement, essentially a tax levied by the nobility on the nobility. In their ownership of token fiefs, the new families exemplify how noble identity paradoxically was linked with immunity from certain kinds of taxes yet also with the obligation to pay another kind.

If in the seventeenth century fiefholding was no longer the sole preserve of traditional nobility, neither was officeholding characteristic only of the anoblis. As I showed earlier (table 1) a large majority of the old noble families in Aix held some royal offices during the period. Obtaining a place in the sovereign courts was often more socially and politically than financially rewarding. Income from these offices was actually rather mediocre when compared with the return on commerce, and those Provençal nobles who preferred to put their money in business did so without risking derogation. The salary, or *gages,* for an office in the courts consisted of interest on the sum

16. Cubells, *La Provence des Lumières,* 116–24.

originally paid for the office, which ranged generally from 1 to 4.5 percent. Kettering calculated the incomes for various offices in the Parlement in 1647. The first president received 2,062 livres; the other presidents made 1,650 livres; and councillors earned 1,225 livres. Parlementaires could also earn income in the form of *épices,* or fees paid for general legal services, and they enjoyed certain legal privileges. For example, parlementaires were not subject to various royal taxes such as the *gabelle,* and they did not answer the *ban* and *arrière-ban.* These assorted benefits, however, failed to compensate for the modest return on offices, especially on those all-too-frequent occasions when payment was not forthcoming or when increases in salary were accompanied by forced loans to the crown.[17]

Yet the demand for offices, and therefore their price, rose tremendously during the seventeenth century. At the beginning of the period the office of councillor in Parlement sold for between 3,000 and 6,000 livres; the cost increased dramatically beginning in 1626, when one wealthy family paid the unprecedented sum of 54,000 livres for the office of councillor. By 1633 the same office sold routinely for 50,000 to 60,000 livres. As Kettering has shown, even given a 60-percent devaluation of the livre-tournois, this shift amounts to a 400-percent increase in the price of the office of councillor over a relatively brief period of time. Prices fluctuated somewhat during the remainder of the century; they fell, for example, after the creation of the Chambre des Requêtes in 1641 and after certain attempts by the crown to lower the costs of offices artificially, and they rose again after the Fronde. By the late seventeenth century, however, prices had generally stabilized at a high level, with the office of president *à mortier* selling for 120,000 livres and a councillorship for 64,000 livres.[18]

No overall inflationary trend accounts for the soaring prices of judicial offices because over the same period other prices in Aix rose only slightly. Consider the cost of that most basic of commodities, wheat. The price of wheat fluctuated dramatically during the years 1600 to 1680 (see graph 1), but most of the ups and downs undoubtedly resulted from natural forces. For example, outbreaks of the plague in 1629 and 1650 explain the price surges following those

17. Kettering, *Judicial Politics,* 225–31.
18. *Ibid.,* 221–24.

GRAPH 1

Price of Wheat in Aix, 1600–1680

*Prices are given in livres per quintal. One quintal equals 100 kilograms.

Sources: ADBR, Aix, B3709, "Rapport de grains, 1570 jusques à 1670"; B3710, "Rapport sur les grains, 1626–81."

years; the epidemics disrupted the harvesting and distribution of grains by reducing the labor force and by causing the inevitable market dislocation that accompanies demographic disasters. The other large price leaps likely reflect the bad weather and poor harvests common to all of western Europe during the period. Conversely, the occasional steep drops in price probably reflect good weather, heavy harvest, and oversupply. In any case, when the zigzag rises and falls are averaged out, the long-term increase in the price of wheat turns out to have been quite small. The average for the last three decades of the period is only 38 percent above the average for the first three decades (see graph 2).

As an economic index, this modest increase over several decades indicates a slow rate of inflation, if not in fact a stagnation. Certainly the price of wheat did not nearly keep pace with the prices paid for offices. The large disparity between the two was caused by the great demand for offices: Kettering found that when the price reached its

GRAPH 2

Decennial Averages of Wheat Prices in Aix*

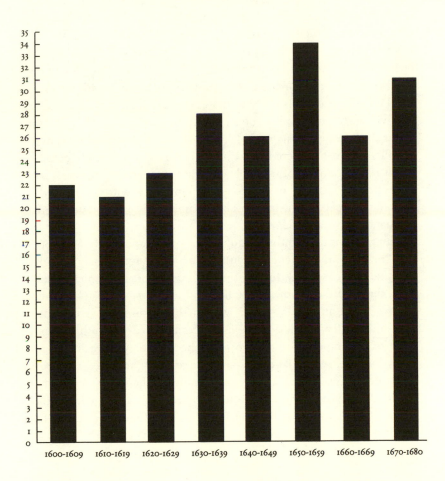

*Prices are given in livres per quintal.

Sources: See graph 1.

highest point, the volume of sales did also.[19] With the abundant ennoblements in the late sixteenth and early seventeenth centuries, the
demand for offices raised the price to extraordinary levels. But this
demand cannot be explained solely by pointing to the increasing
number of anoblis who sought the ennobling properties of offices.
Many old noble families also competed for positions in the courts,
their participation inspired by centuries of service to the community,
by opportunism in their desire to control politics in the region, and
by their recognition of officeholding as a marque de noblesse.

The wealth of both old and new families was therefore invested
similarly in fiefs and offices, and the parallel extends to a third realm
of investment as well—the rente. In Chapter V, I address this investment in greater detail in the context of municipal life, but it should
be noted here that municipal *pensions,* which operated much like the
royal rentes, were an increasingly popular investment with the Aixois. Huppert maintains that the rente was essential to the economic
survival of the anoblis, his "bourgeois gentilshommes." He says that
it was the most easily negotiable form of capital available to them as
anoblis, and that it offered many of the benefits of commerce because
it was really "a form of moneylending at fixed rates." Finally, it had
the virtue of secrecy, hence its great popularity with anoblis who
wished to preserve their fortunes but scrupulously avoided the stigma
of finance and *marchandise.*[20]

Huppert considered this disguised form of moneylending the per-
fect "gentry" investment. Yet in Aix it became immensely popular
with old noble families. In fact, they invested more in municipal pensions than did the anoblis (see Chapter V, table 11). This point suggests once again similarities in wealth that promoted assimilation
within the native nobility. Huppert is certainly correct in his assessment of the importance of rentes, but because they were such a lucrative alternative to land and commerce, they attracted investors
from old houses as well as new. Undoubtedly the urban orientation
of the old Aixois families promoted their familiarity with urban
forms of investment, thereby enabling them to function easily in the
increasingly capitalistic world of the seventeenth century.

This pattern of merging interests between old and new nobles—a

19. Kettering, *Judicial Politics,* 225.
20. Huppert, *Les Bourgeois Gentilshommes,* 141–42.

pattern that will reappear often, with important implications for the structure of aristocratic society in Aix—stands out clearly in the financial strategies of the five extended families on whom I have chosen to focus. The group includes two old families, the Guirans and the Coriolis, and three new ones, the Séguirans, the Beaumonts, and the Mazargues. I chose these five because in their different backgrounds they exemplify the various elements present in the native nobility. An examination of their fortunes will suggest the diversity, range, and results of the investments that Aixois nobles typically made.

Of the two old families, the Guirans were the older—at least, their claims to nobility rested on the oldest document, a royal cavalcade on which the signature of Hugon Guiran, a merchant in Aix, appeared in 1355. Until the sixteenth century the Guirans' history was a typically southern combination of mercantile, legal, civic, seigneurial, and military activities. In the fifteenth century Guillaume de Guiran and his son Pierre managed the family's commercial interests and served as syndics on the town council, while another son, Raimond, joined the order of the Knights of Rhodes and held the position of governor of Tournon.[21]

Like many noble families in Aix, the Guirans had made their fortunes in commerce and land but gradually withdrew from commerce and in its place substituted judicial offices. One eighteenth-century historian wrote that Honoré de Guiran had become by the late sixteenth century a figure of such importance to the Estates of Provence that Henry IV was obliged to pardon his various intrigues with the duke of Savoy.[22] Succeeding generations of the family continued to participate in local and regional politics through positions on the town council, in the Cour des Comptes, in the Parlement, and in the bureaucracy of the généralité.

In addition to their considerable investment in offices, the Guirans owned the fiefs of Fonteverte near Aix and La Molle in the *viguerie* (a judicial administrative unit peculiar to southern France) of Draguignan. According to the 1668 afflorinement, the combined revenues

21. Blanc, *Origines,* 312; ADBR, Aix, MS, Simon-Joseph Barcilon de Mauvans, "Critique du nobiliaire de Provence par l'ordre alphabétique," (N.p., n.d.), 661; B. Méjanes, MS 1133, "Jugement de la noblesse de Provence," 1053; Artefeuil, *Histoire héroïque et universelle,* II, 6.
22. Barcilon de Mauvans, "Critique du nobiliaire," 665–66.

of these two fiefs came to 3,050 livres annually.[23] Unfortunately, the same information does not survive for La Brillane, the family's most important and largest fief; nor is the extent of their allodial property or the exact location of their townhouses in Aix known, although references to several urban dwellings appear in two of the family's marriage contracts. The Guirans were also creditors of several communities; in 1639 they were criticized as one of the three families that had earned 45,000 livres in interest from the community of Barjols.[24]

The city of Aix was another of the Guirans' debtors. Municipal records indicate that in 1649 three members of the family owned pensions or bonds from the city, at a total value of 11,236 livres. Even more revealing of the family's financial practices was the transaction into which Joseph de Guiran entered in 1691. Acting in the capacity of "*mary et maître de la dot de dame Isabeau de Gautier son espouse,*" Guiran received 583 livres from the city of Aix. This sum represented annual interest paid on a 15,700-livre bond that was owned by Pierre Azan. Azan had named Guiran to receive the interest as annual payment for the office of advocate in Parlement, an office previously owned and occupied by Guiran's father-in-law and now part of the estate inherited by Guiran's wife.[25]

This single transaction reveals several important things about the financial practices of the nobility. First and obviously, it shows that old families, like Huppert's "gentry," did indeed function in the intangible world of bonds or pensions. Second, the fact that the interest was traded as payment for an office demonstrates one reason for the appeal of bonds to old and new alike, namely, that they were easily negotiable. Finally, the transaction provides a sense of the financial flexibility of old families like the Guirans. In accepting the annual interest on Azan's bond as payment for an office in the Parlement, they were in effect financing the purchase of that office for him. (As to why Azan, if he were short of ready cash, did not simply liquidate his bond and buy the office outright, this was not possible. An individual who loaned money to the city by purchasing a bond could not demand reimbursement; only the city—the borrower—could choose the time to reimburse. In this respect bonds could be

23. B. Méjanes, MS 1143, "Etat du florinage," 83, 126.
24. Kettering, *Judicial Politics,* 102.
25. AC, Aix, CC289, "Dettes de la ville," 1691–94.

problematic.)[26] Still, the owner could always negotiate a bond in its own right, just as Azan chose to do. By doing so, he was earning interest on a sum originally invested with the city, sufficient earnings to finance the purchase of this office. By their willingness to accept payment in this form, the Guirans demonstrated their familiarity and comfort with what would appear to be a very bourgeois or capitalistic sort of transaction.

How did the return on their diversely invested wealth translate in terms of the Guirans' life-style? In 1659 Pierre de Guiran, sieur de La Brillane and a councillor in the Cour des Comptes, died leaving his estate to his eldest son. The inventory of the estate lists Guiran's personal property in detail, offering a glimpse of the manner in which he lived. His hôtel, located somewhere in the quartier Bellegarde, was furnished with, among other items, eight beds, six bureaux, nine chests, four tables, thirty-five chairs of various descriptions, and two armoires. Its decor included twenty-two paintings, fourteen tapestries, a large map of the world, five chandeliers, a bronze clock, and a large mirror. Guiran served his guests with an assortment of silver plates and utensils and a ninety-eight-piece service of china. His linen closet was outfitted with forty-two tablecloths, both damask and linen, and eighty-four napkins. Among his other personal possessions were two swords, an old suit of armor, two muskets, and two arquebuses. He was also the owner of a library of 106 volumes. These furnishings might seem modest by the standards of the Loire Valley, but Guiran's hôtel, albeit his primary residence, was not his only one. There remained for the family's use the country house at La Brillane, where no doubt many additional items of personalty were located.[27]

Like the Guirans, the Coriolis were ennobled before 1500, and I therefore have classified the family as an old one. They were not, however, among the oldest families in Aix, despite efforts of genealogists to establish as their noble ancestor Marius Coriolanus, who reputedly lived during the Roman Republic. In his eighteenth-century *nobiliaire,* Artefeuil claimed that the Coriolis were among the oldest noble families in Provence, but it is more likely that they were

26. Dewald, *Formation of a Provincial Nobility,* 231.
27. ADBR, Aix, Fonds Lévy-Bram, 303E-564, 1659–60.

ennobled for legal services around the mid-fifteenth century. The earliest document submitted by the family in 1667 as proof of nobility concerned the entrance of Pierre de Coriolis in the order of Saint John of Jerusalem in 1450.[28] Regardless of the exact antiquity of the family, the Coriolis belonged to the nobility of Aix before the arrival of the sovereign courts and rapidly became a house of great political influence.

In 1554 Louis de Coriolis, known familiarly as "Jambe de Bois," was rewarded with the office of councillor in Parlement for having lost his leg in service to the king. In a relatively short time "Wooden-Leg" became a very prominent figure in Parlement, and from then on the family was deeply involved in regional politics. As president à mortier in 1579, Coriolis directed the secession of a group from the pro-League Parlement in Aix and established a rival court at Monasque (which later convened at Pertuis). This rebel Parlement upheld Salic law and supported Henry IV's claims to the throne, for which Coriolis became something of a provincial hero, celebrated by generations of local historians. In 1625 Laurant, his son, was rewarded for his father's deeds and his own service in Parlement with the title of baron de Corbières. Louis XIII also named him counseiller d'état et privé.[29] The king's favor ended rather abruptly, however, because of Laurant's central role in the 1630 Revolt of the Cascaveoux, for which his office in Parlement was confiscated.

By the early 1600s the Coriolis had won general recognition in Provence as a very powerful and influential family; four generations of the main branch occupied the office of president à mortier during the century. In the first part of the period they used this office, their wealth, and their clients to direct Provençal resistance against the expansion of monarchial authority. In 1630 the family assumed a primary role in the Revolt of the Cascaveoux, calling upon the loyalty and service of a clientele that included several friends and relatives in Parlement. Later in the century the family was reconciled to the centralizing efforts of the state, and Pierre de Coriolis-Villeneuve joined

28. Barcilon de Mauvans, "Critique du nobiliaire," 384–85; Artefeuil, *Histoire héroïque et universelle*, I, 282; B. Méjanes, MS 1133, "Jugement de la noblesse de Provence," 1013.

29. Barcilon de Mauvans, "Critique du nobiliaire," 389–90; Artefeuil, *Histoire héroïque et universelle*, I, 285.

the clientele of Baron d'Oppède, first president in Parlement, who was himself acting as a political broker for Cardinal Mazarin.[30]

In addition to offices, by the second half of the century the family's resources included one marquisat, two baronies, and two simple fiefs. As recorded in the 1668 assessment, annual income from these feudal properties alone was 7,900 livres. How much allodial property the Coriolis held is unknown, but family records indicate that they owned vineyards, olive groves, and fig orchards in the vicinity of Aix. They received rents for the bastides at La Ciotat and La Cadière and for some property on the road to Digne, and were creditors of the community of Salon and the city of Aix. In Aix they occupied several dwellings, including a particularly large hôtel, purchased in the late fifteenth century, which was razed following the Cascaveoux affair. In 1645 Honoré de Coriolis, eldest son of Laurant and father of Pierre, received permission to rebuild the hôtel, which still stands near the top of the Cours Mirabeau.[31]

Traditionally, historians might have classified the Séguirans as *grand robe*, for they became very prominent in the Cour des Comptes and their origins were more recent than those of the Guirans and the Coriolis. Their nobility dates to 1501, when Louis XII bestowed the office of councillor in Parlement upon Melchion, sieur de Vauvenargues, as reward for various legal services. The family continued to hold offices in Parlement over the sixteenth century, and Anthoine de Séguiran participated in the anti-League Parlement at Pertuis, for which he later received the office of president *à mortier*. His career climaxed in 1623 when he became first president in the Cour des Comptes; from this point the Séguirans evolved as another leading family in Aix.[32] The key to their social progress lay in their various

---

30. Clapiers-Collongues, *Chronologie des officiers,* 16, 20, 21–22, 24; Kettering, *Judicial Politics,* 170–71; Kettering, *Patrons, Brokers, and Clients in Seventeenth-Century France* (New York, 1986), 75.

31. B. Méjanes, MS 1143, "Etat du Florinage," 26, 28, 34, 69, 70; ADBR, Marseille, Fonds Coriolis, XIVE-95, 1679–84; AC, Aix, CC282-289, "Dettes de la ville," 1659–94; ABDR, Aix, Fonds Lévy-Bram, 303E-224, 1638; René Borricaud, *Les hôtels particuliers d'Aix-en-Provence* (Aix, 1971), 91–95; Kettering, *Judicial Politics,* 166–67.

32. Barcilon de Mauvans, "Critique du nobiliaire," 1041; Blanc, *Origines des familles provençales,* 534; Clapiers-Collongues, *Chronologie des officiers,* 196.

officeholdings and naval commissions. Having served in 1622 as major general in the navy at La Rochelle, and later as lieutenant general in the Levant, Henri de Séguiran succeeded his father, Anthoine, as first president. Henri was also for a period the client of Cardinal Richelieu, who sent him on a rather celebrated inspection of the coastal fortifications in the Mediterranean. Henri's son Reynaud followed a similar course: he served as a commander in the royal navy until he was injured in 1638, then retired to a post as councillor and waited to assume his father's office. When Reynaud in turn died, his heir became the fourth member of the family to occupy the office of first president.[33]

Having devoted a relatively large portion of their wealth to offices and townhouses, the Séguirans never accumulated landholdings as extensive as those of the Coriolis. The main branch of the family owned the fief of Bouc near Aix, but it produced annual revenues of only 300 livres. In 1645 Annibal de Séguiran also acquired the fief of Auribeau, valued at 725 livres annually. The family claimed allodial holdings that included at least one bastide in the environs of Aix. In town they occupied two very grand hôtels, one on the rue Constantin and the other on the rue Adanson, both of which have survived as fine examples of seventeenth-century urban architecture. Like the Guirans and the Coriolis, although on a much more limited scale, the Séguirans invested in the municipal debt of Aix. At mid-century Guillaume de Séguiran owned bonds worth 4,436 livres.[34]

The Beaumont family offers an important contrast to the older and wealthier Guirans and Coriolis and to the very successful Séguirans, in that the Beaumonts represent the poorer and lesser nobility of Aix. Although the office of first president in Parlement conferred personal nobility on Gervais de Beaumont in 1508, he died without heirs. Collateral transmission of his newly acquired title being impermissible, the social status of his relations was not secure until the

33. Kettering, *Patrons, Brokers, and Clients,* 27–28; Barcilon de Mauvans, "Critique du nobiliaire," 246; B. Méjanes, MS 1133, "Jugement de la noblesse de Provence," 1112–14; Clapiers-Collongues, *Chronologie des officiers.*

34. B. Méjanes, MS 1143, "Etat du florinage," 70, 92; MS 733, "Etat et rolle des lettres patentes acquités . . . aux acquéreurs des fiefs de 1626 à 1680," 29; ADBR, Aix, Fonds Berlie, 301E-296, 1679; Borricaud, *Les hôtels particuliers,* 287–88; AC, Aix, CC279, "Dettes de la ville," 1651.

seventeenth century, and even then the royal commission in 1667 condemned the branch at Brignoles as faux nobles. With the exception of Gervais, no member of the family ever held senior office in the courts, and only two served as councillors during the sixteenth and seventeenth centuries. Instead, the Beaumonts devoted their talents and energies to municipal government, their resources no doubt having restricted their purchase of royal office. Their only fief, located near Aix, was assessed at a mere 100 livres annually. In addition, they owned scattered allodial property, most of it in vineyards, and several dwellings in Aix.[35]

Interestingly, the Beaumonts always had money invested in municipal bonds. Throughout the century they were listed as creditors of the city of Aix, and at mid-century their investment amounted to approximately 4,800 livres. Dewald found that in Rouen there was an inverse relationship between the amount of wealth and land on one hand and the amount of money invested in rentes on the other. Families with less wealth and less land chose rentes because this form of investment sometimes brought greater returns and was always easier to administer than land. In Rouen the older the family, the less its investment in urban forms of wealth and property such as rentes.[36] In Aix this was not the case. Like the Guirans and the Coriolis, the other old noble families that held extensive rural properties also purchased bonds. In fact, they purchased more of the municipal debt than did new families. Families like the Beaumonts, on the other hand, undoubtedly perceived bonds as an easy way to increase wealth and thereby promote the social ambitions of the house. The Beaumonts invested consistently in municipal bonds, although the limits of their wealth necessarily limited their investment. In all of this, the Beaumonts resemble the recently ennobled families of Rouen.

The fifth family, the Mazargues, also stood on the lower rungs of aristocratic society, but because of their Jewish ancestry and their steady pursuit of commerce they add an important dimension to this

35. Barcilon de Mauvans, "Critique du nobiliaire," 246; B. Méjanes, MS 1133, "Jugement de la noblesse de Provence," 1112–14; Clapiers-Collongues, *Chronologie des officiers;* B. Méjanes, MS 1143, "Etat du florinage," 46; ADBR, Aix, Fonds Laucagne, 306E-681, 1604.

36. AC, Aix, CC278, "Dettes de la ville," 1649; Dewald, *Formation of a Provincial Nobility,* 117–18.

group. No doubt their rank in the nobility was affected adversely by
their former Judaism (a background, incidentally, shared by a sizable
minority of Provençal nobles). Louis de Mazargues' name appeared
on a list of converted Jews presented to Louis XII in 1512, and it was
his office as trésorier du palais du roi on which the family staked their
original claims to nobility. Several members of the family held offices
as councillors in the généralité and were barristers in Aix. And all the
while the Mazargues continued to engage in trade. In 1604 Jean de
Mazargues, who is described as "écuyer et marchand d'Aix," bought
the seigneury of Chaudol. Over fifty years later a marriage contract
listed as part of the endowment of Joseph de Mazargues, a councillor
and attorney for the king to the siège général, "un fon de marchand."
The exact nature of the Mazargues' commercial interests is never
mentioned, but it is clear that the family still had their hands in business long after ennoblement. Meanwhile, they acquired three fiefs,
the value of which remains undetermined. The family's testaments
and marriage contracts also refer to some allodial properties in the
terroir of Aix as well as several urban dwellings; the value of these
holdings, too, is unknown. Finally, early in the seventeenth century
the Mazargues had a very limited amount of money, just less than
1,000 livres, invested in municipal bonds. Their names, however, do
not appear among the city's creditors for very long.[37]

In spite of the obvious disparity in background, all of the five families' investments were strikingly similar. Although the size of their
fortunes varied, each placed its wealth in the same things: fiefs, allodial property, offices, bonds, and urban dwellings. Of the five
houses, only the Mazargues continued the pursuit of commerce, and
although they were not the only native family to choose that course,
certainly most of the noble families in Aix directed their wealth toward offices or landed property. In Marseille, by way of contrast,
great numbers of families claiming noble status invested much or
most of their wealth in commerce. The reason for this is obvious: as
the great commercial city of southeastern France, Marseille offered

37. Barcilon de Mauvans, "Critique du nobiliaire," 791; B. Méjanes, MS 1133,
pp. 1203–1208; Clapiers-Collongues, Chronologie des officiers; Blanc, Origines des familles provençales, 375; ADBR, Aix, IVB-77, 1656, pp. 601–603; AC, Aix, CC274,
"Dettes de la ville," 1608–1609.

abundant opportunity for investment in commerce.[38] In Aix business opportunities were much more limited, but the courts and royal government provided other, if less lucrative, options. Consequently, the native Aixois nobility, old and new, purchased offices much more often than they invested in commerce, which clearly sharpened the distinction between noble and non-noble in Aix. Ellery Schalk has suggested that in Marseille the distinction between noble and non-noble within the elite was relatively unimportant.[39] The concentration on commerce there contributed to a much more ambiguous social environment than in Aix, where the relative lack of mercantile investment among nobles clarified their posture with regard to non-nobles.

If shared interests and occupations had a cohesive effect on the nobility as a class and were a major factor in the assimilation of new families by old, surely a similar influence was exerted by the nobles' privileged position above the remaining populace. When one compares the incomes of nobles with the incomes of non-nobles in Aix, the real extent of the nobility's wealth becomes apparent. Although documentary evidence is sketchy, assessments for the capitation tax in 1694 survive for the quartier Saint-Jean (see table 4). This district, the town's most populous, was home to many noble families.

The assessments for non-nobles fall predictably in the lower part of the scale. More than half of the non-noble households paid only 5 livres or less, and 88 percent paid 15 livres or less. In contrast, the assessments for noble incomes were generally higher and more widely distributed on the scale. Although 22 percent of noble households were taxed at 5 livres, the remaining 78 percent were scattered across a broad range that peaked with one household paying 140 livres and another 156 livres. The average noble household was assessed at

38. Ellery Schalk is currently studying the elite of Marseille for the sixteenth and seventeenth centuries. In a paper delivered at the 1989 meeting of the Western Society for French History in New Orleans, Schalk described this elite as aristocratic merchants. Marseillaise families that claimed nobility routinely invested in business ventures. In fact, Schalk maintains that the lines between nobles and elite non-nobles in Marseille were not at all clear, and that the difference did not appear to be very important until the period of Louis XIV's recherches. Schalk's paper, "Nobility, Elites, and Absolutism in Marseille in the Sixteenth and Seventeenth Centuries," comes from research that he is doing for a much larger study of the topic.

39. *Ibid.*

TABLE 4

Capitation Assessment for the Quartier Saint-Jean, 1694

Assessment (in livres-tournois)	Number and % of non-nobles	Number and % of nobles
<1	156 (7%)	—
5	1,008 (48%)	33 (22%)
10	325 (15%)	12 (8%)
15	372 (18%)	20 (13%)
20	108 (5%)	18 (12%)
25	58 (3%)	8 (5%)
30	34 (2%)	10 (7%)
35	25 (1%)	9 (6%)
40	9 (.42%)	5 (3%)
45	7 (.33%)	1 (1%)
50	4 (.19%)	8 (5%)
55	1 (.05%)	5 (3%)
60	3 (.14%)	2 (1%)
65	2 (.09%)	—
70	1 (.05%)	7 (5%)
75	1 (.05%)	3 (2%)
80	1 (.05%)	1 (1%)
85	1 (.05%)	2 (1%)
90	—	1 (1%)
95	—	—
100	1 (.05%)	1 (1%)
105	1 (.05%)	1 (1%)
110		—
115	1 (.05%)	—
120	—	—
125	—	
130	—	—
>130	—	2 (1%)
Totals	2,119	149

Source: AC, Aix, CC5, "Registre de capitation, Quartier Saint-Jean, 1694."

around 30 livres, the average non-noble household at around 10 livres. It is important to keep in mind that these assessments were not based on total income. Annuities, pensions or bonds, and various allowances were not considered in the assessments, and in Aix the greater a family's wealth, the more likely it was that they derived revenue from one of these sources.[40]

What life-style would these income levels have afforded the nobility of Aix? Some historians have maintained that the Provençal no-

40. Guy Chaussinaud-Nogaret, *The French Nobility in the Eighteenth Century: From Feudalism to Enlightenment,* trans. William Doyle (New York, 1985), 52.

bility was a poor relation of its wealthier northern counterpart, but there is no conclusive evidence on which to base such a view. More work has been done on this subject for the eighteenth century, a period for which better records exist, and it is clear that in 1788 a provincial noble could live lavishly on a minimum of 10,000 livres a year.[41] An annual income of 10,000 livres was assessed for the capitation at 100 livres that year. A century earlier, 3 percent of the nobles in Saint-Jean paid this much or more (this and the following comparisons assume a similar *rate* of taxation in both periods, although the exact rate for 1694 is unavailable). Those whose incomes fell between 4,000 and 10,000 livres could also live the good life in the late eighteenth century, and no doubt in the late seventeenth century; an income at this level would have afforded a comfortable and spacious home staffed by several servants, and the luxury of entertaining several times a month.[42] In Saint-Jean 23 percent of the noble population apparently lived at approximately this station. Kettering reports, in fact, that a majority of parlementaires had incomes of from 5,000 to 10,000 livres (with net worths of 100,000 to 200,000 livres), indicating the relative affluence of this sizable element in the noble population. These statistics conform with Cubells' findings for the eighteenth century: she determined that half of the parlementaires lived on incomes between 5,000 and 15,000 livres. She also notes the relative affluence offered by these income levels. By Cubells' calculations, 10,000 livres constituted seventy-four times the annual salary of the average rural laborer in 1720.[43]

Among those in Saint-Jean whose incomes fell between 1,000 and 4,000 livres (51 percent), most could still live reasonably well if they managed their money carefully. In 1788, it appears that about 41 percent of the French nobility were in this income range. Finally, for 1694, 22 percent of the noble families in the quarter lived on incomes of 500 to 1,000 livres. Their lives were severely restricted at this "barely decent level." Even allowing for this group, however, one can conclude that nobles in Saint-Jean were not significantly worse off than their counterparts in other provinces. It should also be noted

41. Kettering, *Judicial Politics*, 231; Robert Forster, "The Provincial Noble: A Reappraisal," *American Historical Review*, LXVIII (1962–63), 691.

42. Chaussinand-Nogaret, *French Nobility in the Eighteenth Century*, 52; Forster, "The Provincial Noble," 691.

43. Kettering, *Judicial Politics*, 231; Cubells, *La Provence des Lumières*, 1112–13.

that by 1695 many of the wealthiest families in Aix had relocated in the new and very fashionable quartier Mazarin, a trend that surely siphoned off some of the more prosperous families from Saint-Jean. Still, Saint-Jean was distinguished by its Italianate hôtels and formal gardens, as well as its very large servant population, all of which reflected the life enjoyed by its many noble inhabitants.[44]

What is perhaps most significant in all this, at least in terms of the sword-robe construct, is that regardless of the exact level of income, old and new families got and used their wealth in much the same way. The fortunes of old houses and anoblis alike originated in land or commerce or both, and later included the returns on offices and bonds. Old families bought offices to nearly the same extent as new families, and they invested in bonds even more. Conversely, the purchase of fiefs by anoblis removed an earlier distinction between *nobles fieffés* and landless nobility. In short, old and new noble families put their money in the same things, performed many of the same duties, and lived in the same manner, all of which had a homogenizing effect on their society. Certainly division and hierarchy existed, but they were based on the extent of a family's wealth, on factions, and on politics. At no time in the seventeenth century were two groups separated and recognized by so-called sword and robe functions.

One institution above all others kept this complex social structure flexible and vital. It promoted the assimilation of new families and old, but at the same time, by allying different houses, it encouraged factionalism. That institution, of course, was marriage.

44. Chaussinand-Nogaret, *French Nobility in the Eighteenth Century,* 52–53; Sarah C. Maza, *Servants and Masters in Eighteenth-Century France: The Uses of Loyalty* (Princeton, 1983), 116–17.

III

MARRIAGES AND DOWRIES

According to the crisis interpretation of the French aristocracy, marriage patterns increased the distance between sword and robe because each group refused to marry with families of the other. But the marriages of nobles in seventeenth-century Aix contradict this assumption. Old and new families intermarried so routinely that the anoblis never emerged as a distinct and opposing group defined by function as well as by antiquity. Because having similar sources of wealth and income eliminated many of the other differences between old noble families and anoblis in Aix, antiquity of family, although often a consideration, became a distinctly secondary one when a proposal of marriage promised a financially rewarding or politically strategic alliance, and it grew even less important as intermarriages over time blurred the lines between old and new. Marriage presented families with an opportunity to improve their social, economic, or political standing, and they therefore approached it in a decidedly calculating manner, with much less regard for the emotional aspects of a union than is given today.[1]

External factors such as wealth, social status, and political power influenced a family's choice in partners; internal factors such as number of siblings placed constraints on family resources. New families sought the advantages of association with old; old families were susceptible to offers of large dowries. Political alignments could also join clans of different antiquity. The motives were various and complex, but the pragmatic attitudes of this early modern elite toward

---

1. Lawrence Stone, *Family, Sex, and Marriage in England, 1500–1800* (New York, 1977), 179–91.

marriage inevitably resulted in intermarriage, which in turn played a determining role in the process of assimilation.

By the end of the seventeenth century many old and new families in Aix had signed marriage contracts. Although the most complete genealogy of Provençal noble families does not list all of their marriages, it indicates that as of 1695, thirty of the newly ennobled families (70 percent) in Aix could point to at least one marriage with an old noble family since 1500. This figure does not indicate what percentage of *all* anoblis marriages were with old families, but it does imply that many newly ennobled families aspired to alliances with the older nobility through marriage. Viewed from the opposite perspective, twenty-seven of the old families (73 percent) in Aix married at least one time with anoblis by the end of the century.[2]

That at least 70 percent of the new families married into old families is not unexpected, since anoblis welcomed the opportunity to make their positions more secure by association with established houses. That 73 percent of the old families permitted members to marry anoblis is more surprising, revealing how readily the old nobility accepted and assimilated new families.

The alliances of the five families profiled in this work suggest the uses of marriage in Aix in the seventeenth century. The value placed on a marriage by the families of the bride and groom was usually implicit in the donations made by both families for the occasion. A typical contract began with the names of the couple and of their parents, as well as the social status and occupations of all the individuals mentioned. The remainder of the contract concerned the financial contributions to be made—particularly the bride's dowry, both its composition and the manner in which it was to be paid.

Among 106 marriage contracts entered by the five families during the seventeenth century, only eight fail to indicate clearly the social status of the intended partner. The remaining 97 contracts reveal that the five families usually practiced class endogamy—that is, most of their marriages were with members of the nobility; only 13 of the 97 marriages were to non-nobles. Although the sample is small, it seems likely that other noble families in Aix also married primarily within their class.

2. Artefeuil, *Histoire héroïque et universelle*, II.

By choosing partners overwhelmingly from among their fellow nobles, the five families helped to perpetuate the nobility's separate and elite status. But marriage patterns *within* this urban nobility did not exhibit the same exclusion of rigidity, and therefore did not result in internal stratification. As table 5 indicates, old and new families intermarried routinely. Although somewhat more than half of the Guirans' and Coriolis' marriages were to old noble families like themselves, nearly one in three were to more recently ennobled families. Except for a considerably greater tendency to marry non-nobles, the three new families show a marriage pattern quite similar to that of the old: somewhat less than one-half of their marriages were to families of their own anoblis background, but fully a third were to members of the old nobility. The general situation clearly was open to intermarriage and assimilation, rather than being one of inflexible exclusion.

Nor were integration and assimilation merely the results of chance or close proximity in an urban context. Noble families considered carefully the circumstances and background of the family to which they married a son or daughter. As Lawrence Stone writes, "The choice of a marriage partner concerned both boys and girls and was especially important in a society where there were large financial stakes and where divorce was virtually impossible." The children of nobles married partners selected by their families and rarely dared to question parental judgment. Early modern society viewed marriages based exclusively on romance or on sexual attraction as surely ill-

TABLE 5

Marriages of Old and New Nobles

Classification of Family	Origin of Spouse				
	Old	New	Non-noble	Undet.	Totals
Old nobility (Guiran, Coriolis)	18 (58%)	9 (29%)	1 (3%)	3 (10%)	31 (100%)
New nobility (Séguiran, Beaumont, Mazargues)	25 (33%)	33 (44%)	12 (16%)	5 (7%)	75 (100%)

Sources: ADBR, Aix, IVB, Les Insinuations, 1598–1700; 301E, Fonds Berlie; 302E, Fonds Bertrand; 303E, Fonds Lévy-Bram; 305E, Fonds Vachier; 306E, Fonds Laucagne; 307E, Fonds Mouravit; 308E, Fonds Muraire.

fated, and parental responsibilities included selecting partners for their children based on more practical criteria.[3]

A son or daughter who married without his or her family's consent risked disinheritance, and the parents' right to deprive a disobedient child was confirmed by royal proclamation. Both the Edict of 1556 and, later, the Edict of Blois (which required the publicity of a marriage and made guilty of *rapt*—abduction—anyone who married a minor against family wishes) attempted to reinforce the parents' authority to choose partners for their children.[4] In 1635 Claude de Beaumont invoked his parental right to disinherit his "disobedient and insolent" son for marrying against his fatherly will.[5] The incident evinces a traditional attitude toward marriage that inevitably produced a network of alliances between noble families based largely on financial, social, and political considerations. Because marriage was inextricably bound to matters of patrimony, inheritance, and social status, negotiations were necessarily complex, technical, and calculated.

The dowry that families assigned to a marriage indicated in most cases the value of the alliance and the ambitions of both parties. Wealthier families obviously could provide larger dowries for their daughters, and less affluent families had to offer more modest sums. But social factors added another very important dimension to the costs of marriage: an older family, regardless of its wealth, could usually expect handsome dowries for marriages of its sons to daughters of anoblis because its rank in aristocratic society was ultimately worth a good deal more than its purely material assets; conversely, a new family might be willing to pay an exorbitant price for an alliance that would improve its social standing in the community and in elite society.

In their marriage contracts old and new families alike indirectly acknowledged that female offspring could be valuable social and political tools—a point attested to by the available mean and median figures for dowries offered by the five families for the marriages of

3. Stone, *Family, Sex, and Marriage,* 180–81.

4. Barbara B. Diefendorf, *Paris City Councillors in the Sixteenth Century: The Politics of Patrimony* (Princeton, 1983), 156; James Traer, *Marriage and the Family in Eighteenth-Century France* (Ithaca, N.Y., 1980), 24–25, 33–34. In Chap. 1 Traer offers an excellent discussion of marriage laws in ancien régime France.

5. ADBR, Aix, Fonds Mouravit, 307E-893, 1635, pp. 626–31.

their daughters to old, new, and bourgeois families (see table 6). The two old families, the Guirans and the Coriolis, followed the same pattern: they generally offered much smaller dowries for the marriages of their daughters to anoblis than for marriages with other old noble families. This was common practice among old families; it was typical for them to seek outstanding alliances for as many daughters as money would permit, and then to settle the futures of their remaining girls at a bargain with anoblis. Predictably, the three new families also spent more on marriages with older households than on marriages with anoblis. Particularly striking is the case of the Séguirans, who invested more than three times as much to marry their daughters into old families as they spent for marriages with families of their own background. Of the three new families, the Séguirans were the wealthiest, the most ambitious, and the most prominent. The fact that the Beaumonts and the Mazargues spent less does not mean that those families did not share the same aspirations as the Séguirans; they simply did not have the same resources at their disposal.

TABLE 6

Dowries Given by the Five Families for Marriages of Daughters *

Family	To Old	To New	To Bougeois
Guiran			
Mean	23,750	10,000	
Median	20,000	10,000	
Marriages	4	1	0
Coriolis			
Mean	16,720	4,125	3,000
Median	15,600	3,250	3,000
Marriages	5	4	1
Séguiran			
Mean	32,250	11,300	4,000
Median	34,500	11,000	4,000
Marriages	4	6	1
Beaumont			
Mean	9,000	7,120	4,033
Median	9,000	5,100	2,400
Marriages	1	5	3
Mazargues			
Mean	17,500	13,100	700
Median	17,500	9,000	700
Marriages	2	8	1

*In livres-tournois
Sources: Same as for table 5.

When possible, however, even lesser families such as the Beaumonts and Mazargues invested substantially in their daughters' marriages because daughters offered access to the social prestige, the political power, and sometimes the wealth of other houses. Although the birth of a daughter may often have disappointed noble parents—and certainly there is ample evidence to suggest aristocratic preferences for sons—daughters were not regarded as useless or strictly burdensome relations. Noble families had long recognized that through marriage women could be political and social assets.

Sons, of course, figured differently in a family's marriage strategies. Old families frequently sought anoblis brides with generous dowries as a means of providing for their younger sons and bolstering the financial interests of the family. New families were eager to see their sons marry the younger daughters of old families—despite the stingy dowries that often accompanied this type of arrangement.

The Guirans especially profited from their sons' marriages to the daughters of anoblis. The dowries they received from newer families averaged more than twice as much as the dowries they gained from old families (see table 7). The Coriolis received large dowries from both old and new families, no doubt because their senior offices and their political influence enhanced their appeal to all. In contrast, the Beaumonts and the Mazargues were offered small dowries by both old and new families because they had considerably less to offer the bride's family. Not so with the Séguirans. Despite anoblis status, their position in the Cour des Comptes procured them brides with good dowries even from old families.

The five families' varying interests and circumstances, as well as those of particular nuclear families within each extended one, are revealed by the individual contracts. Nine of the Guirans' contracts were with other old noble families; four were with anoblis; the status of two could not be determined. The single most important alliance concluded by the Guirans was probably the marriage in 1657 of Anthoine de Guiran to Thérèse de Castellane, whose father was the marquis de Grimaud. Her dowry consisted of 30,000 livres, clothes and jewels worth 3,000 livres, and a gift for the groom of 4,000 livres. The marriage also benefited the Castellane family, as the groom was sieur de la Brillane and keeper of the seal in Parlement. In honor of the occasion, Anthoine received a family donation of 100,000

TABLE 7

*Dowries Received by the Five Families for Marriages of Sons**

Family	From Old	From New	From Bourgeois
Guiran			
Mean	16,160	35,000	
Median	18,500	30,000	
Marriages	5	3	0
Coriolis			
Mean	35,175	40,000	
Median	24,500	40,000	
Marriages	4	1	0
Séguiran			
Mean	22,866	9,760	
Median	18,000	10,000	
Marriages	7	5	0
Beaumont			
Mean	7,071	9,150	3,793
Median	6,300	9,000	2,850
Marriages	7	6	7
Mazargues			
Mean	10,500	4,366	
Median	9,000	3,000	
Marriages	4	3	0

*In livres-tournois
Sources: Same as for table 5.

livres. To his bride he pledged an annual pension of 1,000 livres, a gift of 8,000 livres, jewels worth 4,000 livres, and a house and furnishings worth 33,000 livres.[6] Clearly this union was advantageous to all concerned.

Twenty-five years earlier Anthoine's father had received the same dowry of 30,000 livres from his bride. In that case the bride's family, anoblis from Marseille, stood to gain socially from the marriage and therefore offered a dowry that was more than twice the average. Of course, not all of the family's marriages involved such sums; smaller amounts were also common, usually in marriages involving the sons and daughters of lesser branches of the family. Gaspard de Guiran, for instance, gave his daughter a conservative dowry of 10,000 livres to marry Louis de Fortis in 1624. The groom's family was old but otherwise not especially worthwhile as an alliance. In 1689 the family of Anne de Thomas promised only 4,100 livres for her marriage to

6. ADBR, Aix, IVB-78, 1657, pp. 673–78.

Jean de Guiran because the stakes were not high for either family.[7] The groom's father was the *assesseur criminel* to the siège général, and the bride's father was royal adjunct to the same body, neither of these positions commanding tremendous prestige or influence.

Financial motives, whether aimed at conserving or at augmenting family resources, were especially apparent when the Guirans married anoblis. In 1615 Gaspard de Guiran spent only 10,000 livres to marry his daughter to Anthoine de Croze, advocate in Parlement and seigneur of Saint-Martin. If, however, Guiran daughters received little to marry anoblis, their sons expected much more when choosing a mate from the new nobility. For instance, when Joseph de Guiran, son of that same Anthoine de Guiran who was sieur de la Brillane and Venelles and keeper of the seal in Parlement, married Isabeau de Gautier, he received a dowry that included 40,000 livres from the sale of her deceased father's office, 18,000 livres from property in Aix, 11,000 livres in cash, a gift for the groom of 4,000 livres, and finally the fief and townhouse in Aix that the bride had inherited from her father. The Gautiers, an anobli family, chose to invest almost everything they had in this alliance with the main branch of the Guirans; the fact that Isabeau inherited these properties indicates, however, that she had no brothers and that the family was free to concentrate its wealth on one daughter, making her an exceptionally attractive prospect. Certainly it was a fortune well spent. Joseph would one day inherit from his father the fief of La Brillane, the office of councillor and keeper of the seal, 50,000 livres for an annual pension, another townhouse in Aix, and one-half of his mother's estate, all in addition to the donation of 230,000 livres that his father pledged to him at the time of his marriage.[8]

The motives behind the marriages of the Guirans stand out plainly enough, but the strategies underlying Coriolis marriages are even more obvious. Like the Guirans, the Coriolis invested large sums in the marriages of their children to old noble families of at least comparable and sometimes superior positions. When Louise de Coriolis married Madallon de Vintimille in 1624, her father, Laurent, gave her 30,000 livres.[9] Since at this point the Coriolis were embroiled in

7. ADBR, Aix, IVB-52, 1628, pp. 635–40; IVB-50, 1624–25, pp. 301–305; IVB-104, 1689–90, pp. 188–91.
8. ADBR, Aix, IVB-45, 1614–15; IVB-104, 1689–90, pp. 361–63.
9. ADBR, Aix, IVB-50, 1624–25, pp. 680–82.

regional politics but had not yet received the titles of marquis and baron, they gained significantly from this marriage to a family whose members included the counts of Marseille. Vintimille was himself sieur d'Ollieules and baron de Tournes.

In many cases, the situation was reversed: other old families were willing to pay handsomely for a Coriolis connection. In 1622 Honoré de Coriolis received a dowry from the house of Villeneuve-Espinouse that included what would later be the marquisat of Espinouse and two additional fiefs. This marriage allied two families that would participate several years later in the Cascaveoux revolt, and it served both houses politically as well as financially. On the other hand, thirty-seven years later, the same Honoré—by then baron de Corbières—paid only 4,000 for his daughter, Lucrèce, to marry Cosme d'Estienne, who came from an old but politically unimportant family.[10]

The disparity between the two dowries reflects how differently the Coriolis viewed each marriage. By 1659, the year of Lucrèce's marriage, her father held the title of baron and the office of president in Parlement and had nothing to gain from the alliance with the Estienne family, which partially explains why such an important and wealthy house gave a daughter a dowry considerably smaller than the average for the period. Moreover, even the wealthiest families encountered problems when there were several children for whom to provide, and as the father of five sons and five daughters, Coriolis surely could not have abundantly endowed each of the ten. He was not unusual in this regard. Most noble houses had to budget their endowments to younger offspring carefully so as to have more to invest in one or two especially beneficial alliances. Coriolis had chosen to invest most of his resources in his eldest son and universal heir to the family titles and estate.

Implemented through several wills and marriage contracts, the Coriolis' strategy was to amass an even larger fortune and collection of titles for the eldest son, Pierre de Coriolis-Villeneuve. As specified in his marriage contract with Louise d'Oraison, daughter of the count of Boulbon, Pierre's future estate was to include the land and offices of his father and his maternal grandfather, along with 30,000

10. ADBR, Marseille, Fonds Coriolis, XIV-E-14; Kettering, *Judicial Revolt,* 150–181, *passim;* ADBR, Aix, IVB-80, 1659, pp. 787–92.

livres from his mother's dowry. Pierre's unmarried brothers, Louis, François, and Jean, and his uncle, Jean-Baptiste de Coriolis, supplemented this fortune in their respective wills, each man naming Pierre universal heir to his estate. Although Coriolis-Villeneuve's bride brought a cash dowry of only 9,000 livres, she was the widow of Joseph d'Agoult and heiress to his two fiefs. Coriolis was, in fact, the second person to seek this young widow's hand, an earlier engagement to sieur de Roquefueil having been broken by her father for this more lucrative and important opportunity.[11] Through such unions the Coriolis expanded their already considerable holdings, both feudal and allodial, in Provence.

In 1676 Pierre negotiated one of the family's most prestigious alliances by marrying his son, Jean-Baptiste de Coriolis de Villeneuve, to Isabeau de Grimaldi. By this date Pierre held the titles of marquis, baron, and president in Parlement, and for the occasion the Grimaldis paid a dowry of 90,000 livres. As his own father had done, Pierre named his son universal heir to his estate and titles; he also gave him 100,000 livres.[12] The financial stakes of this marriage testify not only to the wealth of both families, but also to the anticipated rewards of an alliance between two of the most illustrious houses in Provence. Mademoiselle's dowry contrasts dramatically with the 4,000 livres that her groom's grandfather paid in 1659 for a marriage with a much less influential and less affluent family.

The Coriolis did not invest so conspicuously in marriages to anoblis. Five of their sixteen marriage contracts were with recently ennobled families, and in each case the dowry they offered was rather meager. Gabrielle de Coriolis received only 1,000 livres in 1662 to marry a young man from a newly ennobled family. In contrast, Marie de L'Anfant, the daughter of another new family, came into a dowry of 40,000 when she married Honoré de Coriolis in 1697.[13] The L'Anfant family would pay the price for its association with the Coriolis, whereas earlier the Coriolis were simply looking for a spouse for Gabrielle, and one whose background would not require great expense. In marriages with anoblis the Coriolis either paid sub-

11. ADBR, Aix, IVB-76, 1655, pp. 714–16; Fonds Lévy-Bram, 303E-376, 1653, pp. 145–50, 633–35, 695–98, 303E-321, pp. 2339–40; IVB 76, 1655, pp. 714–16.

12. ADBR, Aix, IVB-95, 1676–77, pp. 14–19.

13. ADBR, Aix, IVB-83, 1662, pp. 104–106; IVB-108, 1697–99, pp. 231–34.

standard dowries or enjoyed the generous contributions of the other families. They regarded anoblis as a reservoir of suitable husbands for their daughters and of wealthy wives for their younger sons. Their calculated approach to marriage permitted the Coriolis both to secure connections with powerful older houses and to settle the financial futures of younger sons and daughters through alliances with moneyed anoblis.

Newer but very successful families such as the Séguirans plotted their marriage alliances as carefully as the Coriolis. Following their ennoblement in the early sixteenth century, the Séguirans had risen steadily to a position of considerable importance in the Cour des Comptes and in the municipality of Aix. Marriages with old noble families were instrumental in their social progress, and they regularly invested large sums in strategic alliances. For instance, in 1634 Henri de Séguiran, sieur de Bouc, president in the Cour des Comptes and lieutenant general in the navy of Cardinal Richelieu, pledged 36,000 livres to marry his daughter to a member of a cadet branch of the Forbin family. His offer was well above average, for the marriage was designed to promote the interests of the bride's house. This branch of the Forbin family became a main component in the Oppède clientele that dominated Provençal politics at mid-century. The bride's brother, Reynaud de Séguiran, also joined Oppède's circle.[14] Marriages such as this strengthened the ties that linked networks of clients and political allies.

By the same token other families, old and new, more often than not presented substantial dowries for their daughters to marry the main branch of the Séguirans (see table 6), since by the seventeenth century the family was both prosperous and very influential. In 1647 Reynaud de Séguiran married the daughter of an old family in Aix; her dowry came to 75,000 livres. Admittedly, Silvie de Joannis had no brothers and therefore received her dowry as the heiress to her father's estate. Nevertheless, her father's testament gave the estate first to her mother, who then was at liberty to bequeath the estate to the next generation as she chose. She elected to give most of the estate to this one daughter to be used for her marriage to Séguiran.

14. ADBR, Aix, Fonds Muraire, 308E-1389, 1634, pp. 515–21; Kettering, *Patrons, Brokers, and Clients*, 86–88.

Again, the investment was a good one: as his father's heir, Reynaud would eventually inherit the office of first president in the Cour des Comptes, a charge as lieutenant general, the family's house in Aix and its furnishings, and the fief of Bouc. He received a donation of 300,000 livres from his father specifically for the marriage.[15]

When his daughter married Marc-Anthoine d'Albertas, baron de Dauphin, Reynaud de Séguiran offered a dowry much smaller than the one he had received from his wife's family, but nonetheless quite handsome. The alliance with this old family cost him 45,000 livres. Since he had a son and three other daughters for whom to provide, he could not have produced a dowry equal to that of his wife. In 1676 he gave his second daughter less, 33,000 livres, to marry Louis de Thomassin, in spite of the fact that Thomassin was from an old noble family in Aix whose members occupied several important judicial offices. It seems that Séguiran did not have to pledge the extravagant amounts that one expects to find anoblis offering for marriages with old, established families because his own position was secure. Séguiran then married his remaining two daughters to anoblis. He gave Suzanne 20,000 livres for a pension so that she could marry Anthoine d'Aimar, a councillor in the Cour des Comptes; Gabrielle received only 12,000 livres to become the bride of Alexandre de Guerin, councillor in Parlement.[16] These two dowries compare poorly with the endowments of the two elder sisters and underscore the importance of those earlier marriages to the family.

That the Séguirans provided relatively small dowries when their daughters married anoblis is quite natural, especially since such marriages usually involved members of cadet or lesser branches of the family (the main line married almost exclusively with old families). In 1621 the daughter of André de Séguiran, an attorney in Aix, received a mere 4,800 livres to marry the son of a recently ennobled family. In 1653 Jeanne de Séguiran was given only 12,000 livres for her marriage to an anobli. A few years later Claire and Magdeleine, sisters, had still more modest dowries of 10,000 and 9,000 livres respectively; both women married sons of families that had recently

15. ADBR, Aix, IVB-69, 1647, pp. 576–86.

16. ADBR, Aix, Fonds Lévy-Bram, 303E-450, 1673, pp. 907–15; 303E-453, 1676, pp. 654–58; IVB-100, 1683–84, pp. 716–19; IVB-98, 1681, pp. 444–49.

entered the nobility.[17] In each of these cases the bride belonged to a cadet branch of the family.

In contrast to the ambitious matrimonial maneuvers of important anoblis like the Séguirans, the stakes of marriage extended and received by the Beaumonts always reflected their relatively modest assets, both financial and political. Very rarely did a Beaumont marry a member of a wealthy or influential family. The largest dowry received in one of their contracts consisted of 18,000 livres and a testamentary bequest to the bride of two houses in Avignon. The remaining dowries ranked well below this one in value. Meanwhile, the most paid by an older family for a daughter's marriage to a Beaumont was the 13,500 livres offered by Jean-François de Clapiers in 1628.[18] Beyond settling the futures of daughters, old noble families had nothing to gain from association with the Beaumonts. In 1640 the family received only 11,000 livres from Pierre de Durand for his daughter's dowry. To marry this old family, however, the Beaumonts pooled their wealth and endowed the groom, a younger son, far in excess of his legal rights. From his father's estate Joseph de Beaumont received 6,000 livres. His mother contributed 3,310 livres in debts she held on various individuals and communities. But it was his unmarried uncle, François de Beaumont, who was truly at liberty to make Joseph an attractive partner. Beaumont gave his nephew 24,000 livres and promised the couple a place to live in one of his houses. Eight years later the uncle wrote in his testament that Joseph would, in fact, inherit that house as well as a bastide in the area of Du Puy.[19]

In keeping with their undistinguished position, the Beaumonts married with bourgeois more frequently than any of the other four families, and the dowries accompanying these pairings were smaller than those for marriages with nobles; for instance, Jacques de Beaumont gave his daughter only 2,400 livres to marry Joseph Gantes, bourgeois. Surprisingly, the Beaumonts did not receive large dowries when their sons took bourgeois wives, either. Jacques Jantelme,

17. ADBR, Aix, IVB-48, 1620–21, pp. 730–32; IVB-74, 1653, pp. 678–81; IVB-77, 1656, pp. 982–87; IVB-85, 1664, pp. 331–34.

18. ADBR, Aix, IVB-88, 1667, pp. 571–77; IVB-52, 1628, pp. 343–47.

19. ADBR, Aix, IVB-62, 1640, pp. 527–31; Fonds Mouravit, 307E-906, 1648, pp. 682–700.

"bourgeois d'Aix," gave his daughter only 3,600 livres to marry Honoré de Beaumont, esquire. As late as 1676 Jean-Baptiste de Beaumont married a woman from the middle class whose appeal was certainly not financial, her dowry consisting of a mere 3,000 livres.[20]

In none of these instances were the Beaumonts manuring their land with bourgeois gold. There were no social advantages to these marriages, so the family's motives are not clear. Why would a recently ennobled family persist in marrying with the middle class when its own social position was so precarious that one branch was condemned as false nobility in the recherche of 1667? The answer must be that the Beaumont's lowly position in the aristocracy placed them among the least desirable of the possible marriage alliances for other noble families. They could offer very little socially, politically, and in most cases financially to other noble families. Left with few options among the nobility, they occasionally had to look elsewhere for spouses.

The Mazargues fared better in their marriage negotiations. Because they were wealthier than the Beaumonts, they were more successful in securing alliances with established families, even though their Jewish ancestry placed limits on this success. The dowry that Jeanne de Mazargues received for her marriage to Gaspard de Villeneuve in 1617 was 27,000 livres, well above average for that point in the century. Her father, Joseph de Mazargues, was a councillor in Parlement and obviously recognized the merits in an alliance with the Villeneuves, a family that was not only old, but also highly respected in Parlement (the groom would become a very prominent figure in the 1649 revolt).[21] Joseph de Mazargues had already managed one strategic parlementaire connection two years earlier, in 1615, when he settled the future of a younger daughter with the Antelemy family. This important affiliation with a rising anobli house was gained for a modest 12,000 livres. Finally, also in 1617, Mazargues married his eldest son to Gabrielle de Puget, the daughter of the baron de Saint-Marc, who brought a dowry of 18,000 livres, more than one would expect under the circumstances.[22] But then this was

20. ADBR, Aix, Fonds Bertrand, 302E-752, 1628, pp. 290–93; Fonds Vachier, 305E-73, 1631, pp. 179–82; 306E-928, 1676, pp. 1028–30.

21. ADBR, Aix, IVB-46, 1616–17, pp. 272–76; Kettering, *Judicial Politics*.

22. ADBR, Aix, IVB-45, 1614–15, pp. 629–32; IVB-46, 1616–17, pp. 272–76.

no *mésalliance*. As his father's heir, Melchion de Mazargues was entitled to the office of councillor in Parlement and to the fief of Chaudol. And until the death of his parents, he would receive an annual
pension of 800 livres and would have the use of an apartment in his
father's hôtel. The remaining contracts between the Mazargues and
old families involved considerably smaller dowries than that of
Mademoiselle de Puget, and they each involved arrangements by
other families for their daughters to marry less important members
of the house of Mazargues.

The dowries exchanged by the Mazargues for alliances with new
noble families ranged from 1,100 to 12,000 livres. A single exception
arose in 1645, when the same Melchion de Mazargues gave his daughter, Isabeau, a 50,000-livres dowry to marry Lasard du Chaine, who
was from a distinguished parlementaire family and was himself
councillor to the king, and president in the Parlement of Provence.
This was the most important marriage concluded by the Mazargues
in the seventeenth century. In contrast, their smallest dowry was 700
livres offered for the non-noble marriage of Françoise de Mazargues
in 1615 to Honoré Estienne, a merchant in Aix.[23] Like most families,
the Mazargues were willing to pay for marriages that would prove
beneficial, but the majority of their marriages were with nobles of
similar circumstances or with younger children of some of the less
distinguished old houses.

The information in tables 6 and 7 reflects a predictable relationship
between a family's wealth and the average size of its dowries. Not
only did the sizes of dowries vary from family to family, but they
ranged widely within the contracts of a given family. In fact, there
appears to have been little or no effort to achieve equality within a
given family, as indicated by the great disparity among the dowries
of the four daughters of Reynaud de Séguiran. Likewise, Honoré de
Coriolis blatantly favored his eldest son, Pierre, to the apparent dis-
advantage of his other sons and his daughters. This is not, however,
to suggest that all parents bequeathed their property with a total lack
of regard for fairness or equity; nor is it to suggest that all parents were
as calculating as Séguiran and Coriolis. Gaspard de Guiran, for example, left his office as a councillor in the Cour des Comptes to his son

23. ADBR, Aix, IVB-67, 1645, pp. 334–37; IVB-45, 1614–15, pp. 822–24.

André, but then he established dowries of 10,000 livres for each of his four daughters.[24] After favoring one child, some families attempted to create a semblance of equity among those that remained. But even this limited gesture occurred only on those rare occasions when parents approached matrimonial negotiations as a way of merely providing for their children rather than as a means of advancing the house. In the case of Guiran, none of his sons-in-law came from families whose standing in the community was better than his own.

Families regularly selected one son, usually the eldest, and often one daughter, in whom they invested disparately large amounts for the purpose of securing one or two especially beneficial marriage alliances. The endowments of younger siblings were frequently modest compared with those of the favored son or daughter—often just sufficient to secure a marriage within the nobility, but insufficient to do so with much discrimination. In directing their wealth in this way, the Aixois allowed external factors considerable influence over patrimony.

This does not appear to have been the case everywhere. Barbara Diefendorf observed in the contracts of the city councillors of sixteenth-century Paris a considerable effort to achieve some sort of equality among siblings.[25] Dower rights and the rights of parents to dispose of property were, of course, determined by the laws of the region, and there were important differences between the customs of the Ile-de-France and the legal traditions of the Midi. In southern France the legacy of Roman law reinforced the authority of the father, within limits, to dispose of the patrimony as suited the social and political needs of his family. This is not to imply that fathers were chronically insensitive to the financial needs of their younger children, but merely to state that after those needs seemed adequately provided for, most fathers addressed the long-range social and political interests of their houses by strategically investing the excess in one or two favored offspring. The contracts of the five families are testimony in southern France to what Diefendorf has aptly called the "politics of patrimony."

Despite the ultimate authority of the father, the process of raising

24. ADBR, Aix, IVB-40, 1600–1601, pp. 553–56; IVB-43, 1607–10, pp. 952–59; IVB-45, 1614–15; IVB-48, 1620–21; IVB-50, 1624–25, pp. 301–305.

25. Diefendorf, Paris City Councillors, 237, 268–70.

a dowry was almost always a collaborative effort in which family members combined their individual resources, particularly with large dowries. A bride's dowry usually consisted of both a paternal and a maternal donation, and it sometimes included gifts from other relatives. Most of these donations were made in money because parents carefully reserved their land and urban properties for sons. Parents also might supplement a dowry with the return on municipal bonds (*pensions*) or with debts that were owed to them. A husband enjoyed the use of his wife's dowry during her lifetime, but most contracts required that he return the major portion of the dowry to her family if she died before him.[26] This practice of restitution inspired a custom of exchanging gifts in the very likely event of predecease; that is, the groom and the bride designated certain amounts of their personal contributions for the survivor to keep when one of them died.

When Pollixene de Guiran married Louis de Suffren in 1648, her dowry was valued at 30,000 livres. It included a debt of 18,400 livres owed to her deceased father by Jean-Louis de Thomassin, 2,600 livres to be paid upon consummation of the marriage, 3,000 livres due after the first year of marriage, 3,000 livres payable when the mother died, and a wardrobe of clothes and jewelry worth 3,000 livres. The contract stated that Suffren would return the dowry to the Guirans if Pollixene died first. In consideration of this provision, the bride gave him a gift of 2,000 livres.[27]

The dowry of 90,000 livres presented by the Grimaldis for the marriage of Isabeau to Jean-Baptiste de Coriolis-Villeneuve was one of the largest among the five families. She received 50,000 livres from her deceased father's estate and 40,000 livres from her great-uncle. In the contract the Grimaldis requested that half of the dowry devolve to the male issue of the marriage.[28]

When Isabeau de Mazargues married Lasard du Chaine, her parents both contributed generously. Her father and mother pledged 31,000 livres and 19,000 livres, respectively, and made an initial payment of 6,000 livres. The remainder came in annual installments of

26. Gabriel de Bonnecorse de Lubières, *La condition des gens mariés en Provence aux XIVe, XVe, et XVIe siècles* (Paris, 1929), 90–100.

27. ADBR, Aix, IVB-70, 1648, pp. 680–83.

28. ADBR, Aix, IVB-95, 1676–77, pp. 14–15.

9,500 livres and in a wardrobe worth 4,000 livres.[29] Families rarely produced a dowry from a single source, and in most cases they chose to pay it in installments—especially when they had overextended themselves in order to conclude a judicious alliance. Even the wealthiest could not always pay the full dowry at one time, because the family wealth typically was invested diversely in urban and rural properties, in offices, in *pensions,* in personal loans, and occasionally in business ventures. With limited liquid assets, the bride's parents frequently had to pay over an extended period.

Families would often go to great financial lengths to negotiate a profitable union, and the size and composition of a dowry suggest the intentions of a family in entering an alliance. Social and political ambitions, financial considerations, and family size combined in seemingly endless permutations to influence the sizes of dowries, and the study of this aspect provides one way of unraveling a mesh of alliances to reveal the incentives behind them. The patterns that emerge most clearly among the five families are those of upward mobility and of assimilation between old and new. Of the five families, the Séguirans in particular epitomize the social structure of the nobility of Aix. Ennobled in the early sixteenth century, they rose to a position of social and political prominence that drew many old noble families, often bringing impressive dowries, into a network of alliances with them. Their success reveals how the urban environment had eliminated many of the distinctions that might have existed between old and new families, so that anoblis in seventeenth-century Aix had the opportunity to overcome the one obstacle that remained—their lack of antiquity—and to marry regularly with the oldest families in the town. Intermarriage could not entirely erase, but it did ultimately obscure this last distinction.

29. ADBR, Aix, IVB-67, 1645, pp. 334–37.

IV

INHERITANCE AND PATRIMONY

The death of a father was a critical event for any noble family because his patrimony provided the economic base for the standing of the house. The patrimony was literally the family's fortune, and its preservation was essential. In Normandy and other northern regions, the customs of entail and primogeniture forestalled the fragmentation of familial wealth, but in Provence entail and primogeniture never became legal imperatives. In the late nineteenth century the historian of Provence, Charles de Ribbe, wrote, "The *droit d'aînesse* [priority by age] did not exist in the south of France, not even for the conservation of fiefs."[1] Rather than favoring the eldest son, Roman law placed all sons and daughters on the same legal footing, and if a man died intestate, he exposed his family to the economic dangers of partible inheritance. For this reason the individual's power of testament was crucial in the southern nobility's struggle to combat the dismemberment of family fiefs and fortunes.

The power of testament emerged as a basic element in the customs of southern France after the reemergence of Roman law in the late twelfth and the thirteenth centuries, a revival that established written law in the Midi while Germanic customary law remained the basis of jurisprudence in northern France. Specifically, it was Justinian's law that was revived, and as it penetrated the region it profoundly influ-

---

1. Charles de Ribbe, *Les familles et la société en France avant la Révolution, d'après des documents originaux* (Paris, 1873), 505. De Ribbe's interpretation of southern inheritance laws is reiterated by the great legal historian of Provence, Roger Aubenas, in *Le testament en Provence dans l'ancien droit* (Aix, 1927), 123–26.

enced local inheritance patterns.[2] It specified that should a man fail to provide a written testamentary disposition during his lifetime, then upon his death his property was to be divided equally among all his heirs. Thus the only way an individual could combat the progressive fragmentation of his family fortune was by writing his testament, directing the distribution of his property among his heirs after his death. The differences between inheritance practices as they evolved in northern and in southern France are perhaps best explained by Emmanuel Le Roy Ladurie: "The Normans killed off the father. But the Romans, whose law will have such strong influence on the people of southern France, believed on the contrary that the father's wishes survive in this world even when he passed on."[3]

Roman law originally placed very few limits on the powers of the testator, but during the reign of Justinian these powers were circumscribed to ensure a portion of the patrimony for each child. A father nevertheless had the authority to give an advantage to at least one heir; that is, the testament as it was revived in the late twelfth and thirteenth centuries provided a way of endowing one child with the major portion of a family's estate. The patriarchs of noble families, using this prerogative to avoid dismembering their fortunes, developed the common practice of granting an advantage to one child, usually the eldest son. By permitting an uneven distribution of property among heirs, the absolute power of the testament in southern France kept many family fortunes intact, and in designing their testaments to transmit their wealth to one child, nobles in Aix approximated the Anglo-Norman practices of entail and primogeniture.[4]

2. Charles Phineas Sherman, *Roman Law in the Modern World* (3 vols.; New York, 1924), I, 227–28; Aubenas, *Le testament en Provence*, 21–23.

3. Emmanuel Le Roy Ladurie, "Family Structures and Inheritance Customs in Sixteenth-Century France," in *Family and Inheritance: Rural Society in Western Europe, 1200–1800,* ed. Jack Goody, Joan Thirsk, and E. P. Thompson (New York, 1976), 61–65.

4. Jean Yver, *Egalité entre héritiers et exclusion des enfants dotés: Essai de géographie coutumière* (Paris, 1966), 155–56; Aubenas, *Le testament en Provence*, 123–26. For a concise account of hereditary succession in Roman law, see Barry Nicholas, *An Introduction to Roman Law* (ppr.; New York, 1962), 246–58. Paul Ourliac and J. de Malafosse explain the influence of Roman law on southern France in *Histoire du droit privé* (3 vols.; Paris, 1961), III, 299–362, *passim.* Jacques Poumarède describes the reception of Roman law in southern France in *Les successions dans le sud-ouest de la France au Moyen-Age* (Paris, 1972), 72–81. Le Roy Ladurie also deals with the impact of Roman

By the seventeenth century it was common in Provence for a testator to name his eldest son as his *héritier universel*. The universal heir received the largest and most valuable part of the estate, particularly lineal property—the *propres*—which had been in the family for at least two generations. In noble families such property usually included the most important fiefs, titles, and offices. Still, the power of testament did not give families license to exclude completely the other children from the inheritance. The law, having evolved from Justinian's reforming restrictions on the power of testament in Roman law, insisted on the right of all children, sons and daughters alike, to a minimal share, known as the *légitime,* of their father's estate.[5] The légitime was calculated by taking one-fourth to one-third of the total estate and dividing it by the number of younger children. In his testament, a father determined the form of his children's légitimes, that is, whether their shares would consist of equivalent values of money or of land. It was customary for the younger children of noble families to receive their portions in money. If a father did choose to give his younger children land, he generally selected recent acquisitions, the *acquêts,* rather than the more valuable propres.[6] By leaving money to their younger children, most fathers successfully avoided the alienation of lands—particularly the lineal property—from their patrimonies and thus from the inheritances of their universal heirs. The testaments of the five families demonstrate how nobles in Aix used their power of disposition to direct the devolution of their estates with the goals of maintaining a sizable patrimony and, at the same time, providing for each member of the family.

The name of the universal heir almost always appeared in the final section of a will. In earlier sections the testator usually prescribed ar-

---

law on the customs of southern France in his article "Family Structures," 61–65. For an extended discussion of the influence of Roman law in France, see Gabriel Lepointe, *Droit romain et ancien droit français: Régimes matrimoniaux, liberalités, successions* (Paris, 1958).

5. Lepointe, *Droit romain et ancien droit français,* 468. Exceptions, as noted in Chap. III, involved the parental right to disinherit a disobedient child. There were fifteen allowable reasons to disinherit, ranging from physical abuse of the parents to heresy. See Aubenas, *Le testament en Provence,* 80–81.

6. Ourliac and de Malafosse, *Histoire de droit privé,* III, 482; Traer, *Marriage and the Family,* 43. Traer gives an excellent description of the various kinds of property (pp. 41–43).

rangements for his burial and made donations to religious and charitable institutions. Then he parceled out the relatively modest shares
of daughters and younger sons. A husband writing his will did not
always mention his spouse because her claims had often been settled
earlier, in the marriage contract. Having observed the rights of his
younger children, made contributions to charities, and granted special bequests to parents, other relatives, and friends, the testator then
named the heir to receive what remained of the estate. In most wills
the contents of the universal heir's inheritance were not itemized, the
assumption being that the inheritance consisted of the propres and all
property not previously bequeathed in the document.

With the aid of a local notary, Claude de Beaumont wrote his first
testament in 1623, a document that in many ways represents the concerns of most noble patriarchs. Claude began his will with donations
of 30 livres to the local order of Carmelites and 30 livres to a local
church. He then addressed the needs and the legal rights of his family. For his sons, François and Melchion, he apportioned 2,000 livres
each, payable when they reached the age of twenty-five. Two daughters, Catherine and Melchionne, were to receive 3,000 livres each
when they married. For his third daughter, Louise, who was afflicted
with epilepsy and could never marry, Claude established an annual
pension of 150 livres and charged his wife, for as long as she lived,
with Louise's care. An additional clause in the testament concerned
any future children of his marriage; to all male children born after
1623 Claude left 2,000 livres each at their majority, and to all female
children he gave 3,000 livres for their dowries.[7]

As his universal heir Claude named his wife, Pollixene de Gras.
Noble patriarchs frequently chose their wives as universal heirs, particularly in situations where the testator's children were still minors.
Typically, Claude left his wife the use of the estate so that she might
rear and educate his sons until they reached the age of twenty-five
and his daughters until they married. Pollixene was to administer the
estate with the advice and counsel of Claude's brother, Jean-Pierre de
Beaumont. Claude also entrusted her with the responsibility of naming from his surviving sons a single heir to whom the estate would
devolve after her death. He cautioned her to select the most respon-

7. ADBR, Aix, Fonds Mouravit, 307E-882, 1623, pp. 523–27.

sible young man and the one who would most conscientiously tend to the needs of the invalid Louise.[8] By naming his wife universal heir, Claude gave her the financial means to rear his children and still ensured that the estate would ultimately go to one of his sons. At the same time he observed the legal rights of his other children and made certain that his disabled daughter would have constant and adequate care. His testament not only prevented the division of his patrimony by his wife and children, but also established legally his preferences for the fate of the property after the death of his wife.

Like Claude de Beaumont, most patriarchs attempted to preserve the integrity of their estates by naming a universal heir in their testaments. Among sixty-eight wills written by members of the five families, forty-seven belonged to men.[9] Forty-two of these male testators left the major portion of their property to a universal heir. Only four men divided their property equally among all their heirs, and a fifth individual bequeathed his estate to two houses of charity. Twenty-eight of the forty-seven male testators were family patriarchs. All but eight of these family men bequeathed their property directly to one son or indirectly to one son through his mother (see table 8). Moreover, the three men who left their fortunes to their wives with no directions for its succession after her death likely did so assuming that the property would ultimately go to one child.

The single testament that favored a younger son as universal heir over an elder brother belonged to the same Claude de Beaumont. In 1635, twelve years after his first will, Claude executed a superseding document. With his children now grown and himself still living, Claude no longer needed to depend upon his wife's judgment in the division of his estate. He removed her as universal heir and bestowed that honor on his younger son, Melchion. The elder son, François, having incurred his father's displeasure as the result of his clandestine marriage, was completely disinherited. Many years later, however, Claude wrote a third and presumably final testament in which he reinstituted François as his universal heir and consigned Melchion

8. *Ibid.*

9. The sixty-eight testaments of the five families are located in the following collections: ADBR, Aix, IVB, Les Insinuations, 1598–1700; 301E, Fonds Berlie; 302E, Fonds Bertrand; 303E, Fonds Lévy-Bram; 305E, Fonds Vachier; 306E, Fonds Laucagne; 307E, Fonds Mouravit; 308E, Fonds Muraire; 309E, Fonds Lombard.

TABLE 8

Heirs Named in the Testaments of Married Men

Testaments with Universal Heirs	
Eldest son as universal heir	9
A younger son as universal heir	1
Wife as universal heir on condition that estate devolve to one son after her death	10
Wife as universal heir with no stipulation	3
A brother as universal heir	1
Testaments Without Universal Heirs	
Partible inheritance among all sons	2
Partible inheritance among all children	1
Partible inheritance between brother and nephew	1
Total	28

Sources: ADBR, Aix, IVB, Les Insinuations, 1598–1700; 301E, Fonds Berlie; 302E, Fonds Bertrand; 303E, Fonds Lévy-Bram; 305E, Fonds Vachier; 306E, Fonds Laucagne; 307E, Fonds Mouravit; 308E, Fonds Muraire; 309E, Fonds Lombard.

again to the légitime of a younger son.[10] In this testament of 1664, Beaumont did not offer a justification for the change, but it is obvious that relations between the father and elder son had improved appreciably during the intervening years. Perhaps their bonds of affection had been sufficiently strong that, with time and some parental forgiveness, the son's earlier act of "insolence" assumed less importance in the mind of the father. Whatever the reason for this seventeenth-century soap opera, Beaumont's various changes in universal heir imply the value that he assigned to this designation, as well as his desire, even in the midst of familial strife, to preserve the patrimony. Most of the other testators would certainly have understood. The pattern among them is clear: leave as much of the family fortune as possible to a single heir, in most cases a son.

There were, however, occasional exceptions to this pattern, and the testament of Louis-André de Mazargues is a good case in point. In 1626 Mazargues wrote a necessarily lengthy testament to distribute his property among ten children and his wife. He gave two of his four daughters small sums, the balances on 9,000 livres they each had received earlier as dowries. He designated 8,000 livres for a third daughter's dowry, and later raised it to 9,000 livres. His fourth daughter was destined for the convent, thereby limiting Mazargues'

10. ABDR, Aix, Fonds Mouravit, 307E-893, 1635, pp. 626–31; 307E-983, 1664, 360–66.

expense to 2,000 livres, to be received the day she became a nun—although presumbably he had already invested money for this purpose. Then came the bequests to his six sons. To Jean-Baptiste, Honoré, Jean-Estienne, and André went the unspecified amounts of their légitimes. Since the legal traditions of the Midi dictated that sons and daughters receive the same légitime, one can infer that Mazargues' bequests to his four sons were equivalent to the dowries of his daughters, or 9,000 livres. This left two sons and his wife, among whom Mazargues divided his greatest financial assets. For Joseph's *droit de légitime,* Mazargues cited expenses already incurred for his son's legal education and the fact that the young Mazargues would be permitted to live in his house as long as he wanted. What he did not specifically list was his office of advocate in the siège général, which he had just recently passed on to Joseph.[11] Having disposed of his office, Mazargues had only the bastide at Luynes and his house to consider. These he left to his wife, whom he designated his universal heir, directing her to pass the property on to their remaining son, Melchion.[12]

In sum, Mazargues used his power of testament to divide his most important possessions among two sons, giving one an office and leaving the other his real property. One can only speculate about his motives for dividing these properties. Having had the fortune to father six sons, Mazargues, like Honoré de Coriolis, also confronted the overwhelming problem of settling the futures of six young men. This he did for two by placing them in monasteries with their légitimes. One he educated in the law so that the son could then occupy the father's office. Another inherited his bastide and his house. And two were left with their légitimes, to live obscurely under the title of écuyer. Six sons proved to be a mixed blessing. They placed tremendous demands on the patrimony, a situation that was compounded by the needs of four daughters. Given his parental circumstances, it would appear that Mazargues took a utilitarian path, rather than one designed to advance the house. Unlike Coriolis, he provided as best he could for as many as he could. He chose his children over his house.

---

11. ADBR, Aix, Fonds Bertrand, 302E-1004, 1626–27, pp. 423–30; IVB-44, 1611–12, pp. 404–407; IVB-48, 1620–21, pp. 1557–60; Fonds Lévy-Bram, 303E-219, 1631–32, pp. 273–79; Clapiers-Collongues, *Chronologie des officiers,* 346–47.

12. ADBR, Aix, Fonds Bertrand, 302E-1004, 1626–27, pp. 423–30.

As a postscript to the testament of Louis-André de Mazargues, two wills belonging to his son Jean-Baptiste survive. Jean-Baptiste was one of the two sons left only their légitimes and the title écuyer. By 1653, the date of the first testament, he had married and had fathered two children. In the document he named his wife universal heir, with the provision that she pass that position on to the son; he also bequeathed 6,000 livres to his daughter for the purpose of a dowry, or 3,000 if she entered a convent.[13] This latter bequest might serve as an index of Jean-Baptiste's wealth relative to that of his father. Louis-André had been able to produce three dowries of 9,000 livres, to place one daughter in a convent, to give four sons their légitimes (which were presumably equal to their sisters' dowries), to put one son in office, and to leave another his real property. A generation later Jean-Baptiste could offer one of only two children a mere 6,000 livres for her légitime and dowry. Obviously, a significant dilution of wealth had occurred in that one generation. Fecundity ensured the survival of the house, but simultaneously exposed its economic foundation to the threat of serious erosion.

Jean-Baptiste's second will offers a glimpse of family discord and its repercussions in matters of inheritance. He wrote this testament only a year after the first, with the sole purpose of disinheriting his brother Joseph. According to the preceding document, after the wife's death *and* failing Jean-Baptiste's son and any future male grandchildren, Joseph would have become universal heir. In 1654 the testator's only modification was specifically to remove Joseph from the line of succession. In his place he substituted another brother, Honoré, whom he empowered to dispose of the property as Honoré saw fit, with the exception of giving it to Joseph.[14] Although Jean-Baptiste offered no explanation for the change, it was obviously the result of animosity. The timing of the matter suggests a recent and acute disagreement, but it is interesting to speculate as to whether a deeper source of discord between Jean-Baptiste and Joseph was the disparity between their respective legacies from their father's estate. Joseph had received his father's office, not to mention a legal education, whereas both Jean-Baptiste and Honoré had received only their légitimes; perhaps this old disparity played some part in causing Jean-

13. ADBR, Aix, Fonds Bertrand, 302E-1179, 1651–53, pp. 769–78.
14. ADBR, Aix, Fonds Bertrand, 302E-1180, 1654–55, pp. 629–38.

Baptiste to rethink his testamentary plan in favor of his disadvantaged brother.

Even when no direct descendants existed, there was generally an effort to avoid dilution of family wealth. The testaments written by single men, most of whom were clerics or members of chivalric orders, reflect this intent. The property of most single men devolved collaterally to brothers, sisters, or nephews, and some men left their estates to their mothers, but almost always a universal heir was named. Eighteen of nineteen unmarried testators left their properties to relatives, and all but one of the eighteen named a universal heir rather than partitioning properties among several individuals. The sole member of the group who chose to ignore consanguineous bonds altogether was Jean de Coriolis, a priest. His testament directed that three-fourths of his estate go to a poorhouse in Aix and one-fourth to a hospital for the purpose of freeing and, if necessary, reconverting Christians taken as slaves by Barbary pirates.[15]

The remaining testaments belonged to women, and seventeen of twenty-one of them designated universal heirs. Since the economic position of the family did not rest on a woman's property, she was free to concentrate her wealth on individuals other than her sons. In fact, often she disposed of her property during her lifetime by contributing to the dowries of her daughters. As described in Chapter III, the dowries of most young women consisted of both a paternal and a maternal donation, and it was not uncommon for the wealth of the mothers to prove crucial in negotiations of valuable alliances. By channeling her property into the dowries of her daughters, a mother could become a very important player in the family's strategy for social and political progress.

Whether or not they donated to endowments during their lifetimes, women almost always retained enough property to necessitate testamentary requests, and most adopted the practice of instituting a universal heir. Their choices of universal heirs included husbands, mothers, children of either sex, and grandchildren. Mothers often specified that testamentary bequests to daughters and granddaughters were to be used for dowries, perhaps making possible more judicious alliances. Because the preservation of her estate was not usually essential to the family's honor, a woman had the option of reserving

15. ADBR, Aix, Fonds, Mouravit, 307E-963, 1663, pp. 636–41.

less of her wealth for her universal heir and using more of it to make bequests to a greater variety of individuals. In 1637, for example, a Jeanne de Séguiran (not the same as on page 56) named her husband, Pierre de Laurens, universal heir. She began her extended list of bequests in the customary way by leaving 100 livres to the church where she was to be buried, with the stipulation that thirty-three masses be said for the remission of her sins. To the local orders of Oratorians, Capuchins, and Augustinians she gave 30 livres each, again on the condition that they celebrate thirty-three masses for her soul. Then Jeanne named her chambermaid, who was to receive 30 livres and most of her clothing. She also left 30 livres to her cook and 15 livres to another female servant. Sixty livres each went to her husband's clerk, her grandson, and her granddaughter. Her mother who presumably did not need the money, received a token sum of 30 livres. To her children Henry, Anthoine, Jean-Anthoine, and Suzanne de Laurens, she gave 1,200 livres each; her other daughter, Félicité, received 3,000 livres expressly for her dowry. What remained of Jeanne's estate devolved to her husband and universal heir.[16] This kind of latitude in choice, both in terms of the number of bequests and the individual selected as universal heir, constituted the primary difference between the testamentary affairs of the sexes. A woman's bequests could complement the testament of her husband, making the devolution of women's property a matter of great consequence to their families.

Moreover, women could play a subtle but still important role in the devolution of family wealth by influencing the decisions of their husbands and sons. Women routinely participated in the composition of dowries, and certainly on occasion they contributed to the selection of a universal heir. The testament of François de Guiran delegated to his mother a substantial prerogative over his patrimony. Written in 1662, the document named the testator's brother, Jean, universal heir to the family's fief and François' office as councillor in the Cour des Comptes, provided that Jean did not marry without the consent of their mother, Claude de Gaillard. If she refused to approve Jean's choice of spouse, the property would then pass to their cousin Anthoine. Failing Anthoine, it would devolve to their cousin in Normandy, and if *he* should refuse to live in Provence, the prop-

16. ADBR, Aix, Fonds Mouravit, 307E-895, 1637, pp. 232–36.

erty would go to the eldest male child of the testator's daughter.[17] The most interesting provision in this rather complex chain of succession is the right of the mother to disinherit the universal heir from the considerable patrimony of her husband and elder son. Empowering the matriarch to remove a son and substitute a cousin, this document at the very least raises the possibility of maternal influence in the devolution of some patrimonies.

Not only did family members—patriarchs, bachelors, and women alike—almost always choose a universal heir to their wealth, but sometimes relatives channeled their property to the same individual. Ideally, the person so chosen would inherit a strong base on which to maintain the family's social and political position. Through this tactic the relatively small estates of women and unmarried men contributed more to the prestige of the family than would otherwise have been possible. The Coriolis illustrate this sort of cooperation among siblings in their effort to endow one brother, Pierre de Coriolis-Villeneuve, with impressive wealth and an assortment of titles and offices.

Pierre's good fortune was discussed briefly in Chapter III in connection with his marriage. To recap and expand on the matter, in addition to being his father's principal heir, Pierre received through his parents' marriage contract all the property of his maternal grandfather, including what would later be the marquisat of Espinouse. Moreover, three of his four brothers and his uncle all coordinated their wills to bequeath him a still larger estate. The testaments of his unmarried younger brothers, Louis, François, and Jean de Coriolis, each named Pierre universal heir. The fourth brother Laurens, was in the process of entering a religious order in 1656. Laurens gave the usufructs of his property, forty charges of land held in fief (a *charge* being an archaic and highly imprecise, if versatile, unit of measurement), to Pierre on the condition that Pierre contribute to his support annually. After Laurens' death, Pierre would inherit his land outright. Finally, the uncle, Jean-Baptiste de Coriolis, prieur de Grambois, also left his estate to Pierre.[18] By combining their small individual estates, their légitimes, with the patrimonies of Honoré de

17. ADBR, Aix, Fonds Lombard, 309E-1321, 1662, pp. 1608–28.

18. ADBR, Marseille, Fonds Coriolis, XIVE-14; Aix, Fonds Lévy-Bram, 303E-376, 1653, pp. 145–50, 633–35, 695–98; Fonds Lévy-Bram, 303E-321, 1656, pp. 2339–40; IVB-77, 1656, pp. 310–17; Fonds Lévy-Bram, 303E-377, 1654, pp. 790–93.

Coriolis and Pierre's maternal grandfather, Pierre de Villeneuve, Pierre's brothers and uncle helped to build an impressive fortune for the son who bore the family titles.

To ensure that there would be no dispersal of all this wealth in the event that he should die unmarried and childless, Pierre in 1654 made his first will, naming his uncle, Jean-Baptiste, as universal heir. He further specified that following his uncle's death, the fortune would go intact to one of his brothers to continue the "honor and glory of the house." In 1655 Pierre married Louise d'Oraison, and their marriage contract stated that his property would henceforth devolve successively to their male children.[19]

The Coriolis' strategy offers almost a textbook example of how noble families in Aix used, or tried to use, the power of testament not only to prevent the fragmentation of patrimonies, but to strive continually to augment them. Families planned their testamentary practices with great care, aiming to guarantee that the economic base for their standing in Aix would be strengthened by the concentration of wealth through inheritance, not weakened by its dispersion.

Many families planned with equal care when it came to their political standing—for example, of prime value in the vast inheritance of Pierre de Coriolis-Villeneuve was the office of president in Parlement bequeathed him by his father. Royal offices were a popular investment, one that brought power and prestige to old and new families alike, and they often played an important role in the testamentary schemes of the nobility. During the seventeenth century, 77 of the 211 councillors in the Parlement of Provence, or more than one-third, inherited those positions from their fathers. The same was true of the Cour des Comptes: 32 of 104 counselors in the court, or 31 percent, left their offices to their sons. As has already been noted, four generations of universal heirs in the Coriolis family occupied the office of president in Parlement. Similarly, the office of president in the Cour des Comptes devolved to four successive universal heirs in the Séguiran family.[20]

In 1678 Reynaud de Séguiran, first president in the Cour des

19. ADBR, IVB-76, 1655, pp. 714–16.
20. Clapiers-Collongues, *Chronologie des officiers*, 16–24, 19–97, and *passim;* Kettering, *Judicial Politics*, 166–67.

Comptes and sieur de Bouc, died, leaving four daughters, a wife, and a minor son. Shortly before his death, Reynaud wrote his testament to ensure that one day his son, Joseph, would inherit his property and his office. Reynaud arranged for his brother, Anthoine, abbé de Guitres in Guyenne, to serve as guardian by occupying the office of first president until Joseph was old enough to assume that position. Meanwhile, Anthoine composed his own will, naming Joseph as his universal heir. In this way Anthoine took extra precautions to ensure that if he died before giving the office to Joseph, his nephew would inherit the position at his majority.[21]

Although the major portion of a family's wealth, especially real property and royal office, was usually reserved for the universal heir, some provision had to be made for any remaining children. Younger sons almost always received money as their droit de légitime. Among the twenty-four fathers who named universal heirs (table 8), nineteen also had younger sons for whom to provide, and in eighteen cases the younger sons received légitimes in money rather than in land. Such bequests proved useful in purchasing careers in the Church, in chivalric orders, in the army, and in royal government. If a son reached the age of twenty-five before his father's death, he usually received his légitime in the form of an *inter vivos* gift. The father might still provide a token sum in his testament, but the son had no further claim to his father's estate. Claude de Séguiran's will, for instance, left only thirty livres to his son Claude-Annibal, who had previously received his légitime in a donation so that he could enter a monastic order. This practice was known as *exclusion des enfants dotés,* and although it was widespread in southern France, its origins remain unknown.[22] The right of exclusion was important for noble families because it enabled a father who had satisfied the financial rights of a particular child during his lifetime to omit that child from his testament, thereby reducing the demands on his universal heir.

The exclusion des enfants dotés applied to daughters as well as to younger sons. Roman law had provided for equal division of the fa-

21. ADBR, Aix, Fonds Lévy-Bram, 303E-454, 1677–78, pp. 487–90; ADBR, Aix, Fonds Lévy-Bram, 303E-457, 1683–84, pp. 326–28.

22. Fonds Lombard, 309E-1070, 1622, pp. 965–69; Yver, *Egalité entre héritiers,* 24–27; Bonnecorse de Lubières, *La condition des gens mariés,* 139.

ther's estate among all siblings, male and female, and a daughter had the same droit de légitime as her brothers. In the seventeenth century these obligations were customarily met by a dowry for marriage or a donation so that she could enter a convent. Daughters who had already received dowries were excluded from or given only small amounts in their fathers' wills, but their dowries must have been equivalent to a légitime.[23] One approach frequently employed in marriage contracts was to pay a dowry in installments, with the final payment made after the father's death. Whether through her marriage contract or through his testament, a father almost always paid his daughter's légitime in money. Of twenty-one patriarchs with daughters, none bequeathed a daughter land, and most of the wills stated explicitly that money was to constitute either her légitime or the final payment on a dowry agreed upon earlier. A father, of course, could supplement his daughter's légitime by increasing her dowry. Parents often elected to give a particular daughter a dowry larger than the légitimes of other children because a handsome dowry, one that exceeded a légitime, might secure for the young woman's family a strategic marriage alliance. There were obvious benefits to such alliances, and fathers regularly pledged more to one daughter's dowry in the interest of the house. Nine of the twenty-one fathers gave one daughter a dowry that exceeded the légitimes of their other children.

A wife's claim to the estate of her husband was settled in the couple's marriage contract. Most contracts contained a clause promising the wife restitution of the major portion of her dowry when her husband died. In many contracts, too, the husband pledged to his bride an income from *pensions* and use of the family home following his death, as long as she did not remarry. With a wife's rights to his estate clearly established by legal contract prior to marriage, a husband did not have to provide a bequest in his testament. Almost all of the husbands studied, however, added to their pledges of support with testamentary legacies. In only four of the twenty-eight testaments did husbands fail to mention their wives, and in two of those cases the omission was due to the fact that the wives had died first. Although carefully constructed to preserve the patrimony, testaments were not composed with a total absence of emotion. After

23. R. W. Leage, *Roman Private Law* (London, 1948), 181.

years of marriage, husbands were often moved to provide for their spouses in excess of their legal obligations.

Of the twenty-four husbands who did provide for their wives in testaments, two promised only the restitution of their dowries. Another, Reynaud de Séguiran, simply required that his son and universal heir, Joseph, house and feed his mother as long as she lived. The testaments of four were more detailed and generous, leaving houses, annual *pensions,* and specific sums of money to their widows. Four other husbands left their wives in even more secure circumstances by giving them the usufructs of their estates; that is, their wives enjoyed for life the use of their husbands' property, but did not have permission to alienate it in any way, since it was reserved ultimately for the person named universal heir. The testaments of thirteen noblemen took the ultimate step and named wives as universal heirs; again, however, a wife who inherited the estate of her husband usually did so on the condition that she in turn leave it to the eldest son (or, sometimes, to the son of her choice).

Husbands, then, provided for their wives in a variety of ways, but overall the testaments of these noblemen reveal a genuine concern for the financial futures and the physical maintenance of their wives, a sentiment that suggests more than mere fiscal and marital responsibility. Such bequests, like that of Claude de Beaumont for the care of his invalid daughter, are certainly the results of an emotional bonding within the early modern family that is generally overlooked by social historians. Husbands and fathers were not motivated exclusively by the desire to preserve the economic base of the house. Emotion could and often did influence testamentary arrangements, usually with the effect of complicating them.

The concerns of a noble patriarch for the financial future of his family and the fate of his house were demanding and sometimes conflicting. In the balance hung the family's social and economic position and the needs and legal rights of its children. A father had to provide some income for all of his children, while trying at the same time to enhance the family's standing by maintaining its fortune intact. Through skillful use of their testaments and marriage contracts, noble families avoided the ruinous custom of partible inheritance and still provided for all their members. The death of the father might bring emotional instability and a change of authority to a noble household in seventeenth-century Aix, but it did not necessarily bring financial instability as well. A father's desires for the fate of his property survived him in his testament, and most noble patriarchs used this power successfully to direct the transmission of their fortunes in the interest of the "honor and the glory of the house."

V

MUNICIPAL LIFE AND CIVIC HUMANISM

In contrast with their northern counterparts, and owing to the circumstances provided by their urban location, the nobles of Aix in many of their activities resembled an Italian patriciate. Like the *grandi* of an early Renaissance city-state, these families thoroughly infiltrated and controlled the various arenas of municipal life. This was only natural: the history of noble participation in the community was, after all, an ancient one, originating with the Roman custom of service, evolving during the Middle Ages to include a defensive capacity, and maturing under the influence of civic humanism and the Counter-Reformation to include a sense of noblesse oblige.

The nobles of Aix continued to observe the Roman tradition of service to the community and state by participating in the political life of the town. As captains of their quarters and commanders of citizen militias, they preserved the medieval function of providing defense. And in assuming much of the burden of charity, they found expression also for a more modern sense of obligation and service to the community. When visitors in the seventeenth century referred to Aix as a "ville aristocratique," they gave contemporary recognition to the preponderance and hegemony of noble families there. Of course, the presence of the sovereign courts had significantly swollen the town's noble population by attracting numerous officeholding families who were not native to Aix—although many of them participated energetically in municipal life. But at the heart of the elite and at the center of its municipal institutions were the native noble families whose devotion to their urban community stemmed from

79

centuries of tradition. The description "ville aristocratique" implies more than numbers; it connotes a heritage of aristocratic involvement, and suggests that this heritage was to a certain extent unique.

Local government in Aix was elective, with the principal power residing in the town council. Nominations for offices were drawn from each of the five *quartiers* of the town. As a result, aristocratic power in local government depended in large measure on demographic distribution within the town, and indeed, the nobility was not exclusively domiciled in any one quarter. Although there was some concentration in the southern neighborhoods, aristocratic elements were spread throughout the community, a situation that made for a complex mixture of classes by both quarter and street. It was quite possible for the humble residence of an urban craftsman to sit adjacent to the grand hôtel of a marquis. Coste's work confirms this dispersion, with only the faubourg housing a negligible noble population—and residents of the faubourg did not participate in the electoral process. In areas that were important in town politics, the aristocratic presence was conspicuous, the favored residences being the tall, spacious hôtels that reflected the Italian influence on Provençal architecture and decorative arts. To distinguish their townhouses from similar residences belonging to wealthy bourgeois, and to emphasize their own separate and privileged place in urban society, nobles proudly marked their buildings with coats of arms. Coste determined that in 1695 there were 192 residences of this sort in the five quarters. They were liberally, if not equally, distributed: 69 in Saint-Jean; 54 in Augustins; 21 in Cordeliers; 27 in Bellegarde; and 21 in the Bourg.[1]

Given the nature of the electoral process in Aix, the nobles' geographic distribution offered them a broad base of power. To have concentrated in a single quarter, as is often characteristic of elites, would have limited much of their political influence to that quarter and would have drastically reduced the total number of positions they could occupy in local government. In this sense, political power in the municipality was a simple matter of demographics, which, as it happened, played into the hands of the nobility. As in many Mediterranean towns, the town council was headed by three consuls and

1. Carrière, *La population d'Aix-en-Provence*, 96; Coste, *La ville d'Aix en 1695*, I, 62–65, II, 1036–51.

an assessor, who were elected each September by a rather complex procedure. The electoral process began with nominations for the consulate from a committee composed of the incumbents and the former consuls and assessor from the previous year. The nominations were presented to a special election assembly that included the nominating committee, the thirty councillors-elect, the sixty present councillors, the treasurer, the five captains of the guard, and the "abbé" and the "prince d'amour" (both of whom were elected by the council to preside over the Fête Dieu during Pentecost). This assembly then approved or rejected the slate of nominees, and since substitutions were not allowed, real control of elections rested with the nominating committee.[2]

The thirty councillors-elect—the *cités,* as they were known—had been selected the day before by lot for two-year terms from a list of one hundred notables, twenty from each quarter. The one hundred having also been nominated by the committee of incumbent consuls and assessors, the system was what Kettering has described as a "self-perpetuating" aristocratic oligarchy. The thirty new councillors joined the thirty elected the previous year, forming a new council of sixty. A similar situation existed in sixteenth-century Paris, where city government was dominated by a nucleus of interrelated families acting in a tradition of civic service.[3]

The local nobles' demographic dispersion within the town permitted them to dominate the town council and municipal politics, but their control of the consulates was even more crucial to their control of municipal affairs. As the highest representatives of communal activity, the consuls and the assessor commanded great prestige and authority both within the town walls and beyond. In addition to their municipal functions, the consuls and the assessor served as *procureurs du pays,* or as the executive committee of the Estates of Provence—a fact that made these positions rather strategic in the provincial nobility's efforts to resist the intrusion of royal authority in the first half of the seventeenth century.[4] Because of this regional component of the office, the membership of the consulates was not exclusively Aixois. Many nobles who had only recently located to

2. Kettering, *Judicial Politics,* 41–42; BDR, XIV, 513–521.
3. Kettering, *Judicial Politics,* 42–44; Diefendorf, *Paris City Councillors,* 41.
4. BDR, XIV, 529; Kettering, *Judicial Politics,* 42.

Aix also participated in municipal institutions, particularly in the consulates, thereby gaining access to the positions of procureurs du pays. Of course, consuls possessed considerable municipal powers as well, the consulate having acquired in 1547 the right to pass ordinances for the town. Furthermore, the body's police powers were sufficient to provoke repeated jurisdictional conflicts with the intendant and with the Parlement.[5]

Custom prescribed that the first consul belong to the fiefholding nobility of Provence, that the second be a member of the local nobility, and that the third come from "la bonne bourgeoisie." The assessor, who shared administrative power with the consuls, was chosen from among the attorneys in Aix.[6] Custom thus gave nobles a theoretical numerical advantage within the consulate of two to one. In practice their advantage often exceeded this because many of the third consuls were also nobles; moreover, by the seventeenth century most of the assessors were nobles trained in law.[7] Altogether, nobles held 298, or 77 percent, of the positions in the consulate between 1598 and 1695 (see table 9). Of these seats, 137 were occupied by members of the native noble families.[8]

The fact that incumbents nominated their successors was the source not only of the nobility's numerical preponderance, but also of fierce factionalism. Patrons could place their clients as consuls, assessors, and councillors simply by nominating them. This leverage permitted great nobles like the Forbins to annex city government and augment the power they wielded through the sovereign courts and the généralité.[9] Municipal government inevitably became a battleground for rival factions, and at no time was this rivalry more visible than during the annual elections, when competing factions contrived

5. BDR, XIV, 531.

6. BDR, XIV, 532; Allemand, *La haute société aixoise,* 101–102; Kettering, *Judicial Politics,* 42–43.

7. Kettering also notes this discrepancy between what the law prescribed and what in fact took place in the selection of the consulate, which generally gave the nobility an advantage of three to one. See *Judicial Politics,* 44.

8. The native noble families serving on the consulate for this period break down as follows: 33 first consuls (30 from old families and 3 from new), 64 second consuls (30 from old families and 34 from new), 7 third consuls (4 from old families and 3 from new), and 33 assessors (17 from old families and 16 from new). AC, Aix, BB130, *Catalogue des consuls et assesseurs de la ville d'Aix* (Aix, 1799), *passim.*

9. Kettering, *Judicial Politics,* 44.

TABLE 9

Social Origins of Consuls and Assessors, 1598–1695

Office	Nobles	Non-nobles	Totals
First Consul	97		97
Second Consul	97		97
Third Consul	29	68	97
Assessor	75	22	97
Totals	298	90	388

Source: AC, Aix, *Catalogue des consuls et assesseurs de la ville d'Aix* (Aix, 1799), 30–44.

to influence the nominations of friends, relatives, and clients. In 1651, 1653, and 1654, for example, Henri de Forbin-Maynier, baron d'Oppède, used the municipal elections to place his relatives and partisans in control of the consulate, the council, and therefore the positions of the procureurs de pays. He did so at the expense of the clients of Charles de Grimaldi, marquis de Régusse, with whom he had been competing for the coveted patronage of Cardinal Mazarin. By dominating the elections, Oppède demonstrated to Mazarin the extent of his political influence and *credit,* thereby persuading Mazarin of his potential value as a client and broker of ministerial patronage.[10] (Chapter VI describes Oppède's rise to power, his role as a broker, and his contribution to the political integration of the local nobility in the emerging absolutist state.)

In 1659 the factional intrigues in municipal elections became so scandalous that the king himself intervened. The nominees of 1659 were revoked and a new consulate declared by the king's agents on the grounds that the earlier election had taken place under duress; that same year, the crown attempted to curtail factional disputes and to limit the nobility's influence by insisting that henceforth one-half of the councillors be bourgeois. It has been suggested that much of the friction and factionalism that colored municipal politics and municipal life in Aix saw sides drawn according to the antiquity of the families involved; that is, the old nobility attempted to exclude new families from office. Yet a sampling of the rolls of the town council for every fifth year during the century reveals the names of 65 noble families, of which 31 were old and 34 new. Only 7 old families and 9

10. Kettering, *Patrons, Brokers, and Clients,* 47; *Judicial Politics,* 299.

new families failed to serve.[11] During these five-year intervals, old and new families occupied almost equal numbers of positions on the council—old families held 119 seats and new families 114. Thus, it would seem that although factionalism may have shut certain families out of municipal government, lack of antiquity as such did not.

Each of the five families had members who were councillors at some point in the seventeenth century, and all but the Mazargues had representatives in the consulate at various times. Honoré de Guiran and Honoré de Coriolis both served as assessors in the early part of the century, and Jean-Louis de Coriolis became first consul in 1625. But it was the Séguirans and the Beaumonts whose members were nominated to these positions most often. Séguirans held the office of assessor five times and the office of second consul six times; Beaumonts succeeded to the office of second consul seven times and the office of third consul once. A complete accounting of the five families' participation on the council, including the years that members held positions as councillors, appears in Appendix III.[12]

Séguirans appear on the rolls of the council for forty-one years of the century, the Beaumonts for sixty-seven years. This longevity helped the families create a quasi-monopoly that reinforced the self-perpetuating aspects of local government. Rather modest financial assets no doubt restricted the Beaumonts to the town council in search of political influence. But the Séguirans held several senior positions in the Cour des Comptes in addition to their many offices in municipal government, a fact that suggests the two spheres were not mutually exclusive—that power in the courts did not preclude an interest in local politics. Royal offices were venal and in one sense represented an investment for the family; municipal offices were elective and incorporated a degree of civic humanism and duty to the urban community. But both spheres offered families access to political power. Southern nobles had been governing their urban communities since the rise of town councils and consulates in the early

---

11. Marcel Bernos, "Aix au grand siècle," in *Histoire d'Aix* (Aix, 1977), 146; Kettering, *Judicial Politics*, 45–46; AC, Aix, BB99-105, "Délibérations du Conseil," 1600–95. In sampling the council records, I used the minutes of the first meeting of every fifth year during the period 1600–1695. The first meeting being the one at which new members were chosen, it was the best attended.

12. AC, Aix, BB130, *Catalogue des consuls*, 30–44.

Middle Ages, which was only natural, for the town was their primary residence and they in turn were its leading citizens. At least in part the descendants of a Gallo-Roman aristocracy, early medieval elites also preserved the classical custom of aristocratic service to the state, a custom that was to a certain extent restated by the humanists, who found virtue in the active rather than the contemplative life.[13] Control of municipal offices was therefore as essential to this urban elite as control of royal offices was to the French nobility as a whole.

Local aristocrats not only participated in municipal government, but also funded it through the purchase of *pensions*. These municipal bonds operated like royal bonds, or *rentes sur l'Hôtel-de-ville* in Paris, in that an investor loaned to the local government a sum of capital for which he or she received 5 percent annually in interest. Rentes became a very popular form of investment with the French aristocracy, but the Aixois, so fiercely loyal to their *pays*, preferred to put their money in the local bonds rather than in the royal rentes.[14] Families frequently left *pensions* to their heirs or gave them in marriage contracts because the investment offered a relatively safe means of providing at least a small annual income for relations, especially wives and daughters, in the absence of the patriarch. *Pensions* were also a good way to endow a church, confraternity, or charity.

In general terms noble investment in the municipal debt of Aix increased over the course of the seventeenth century. Indeed, the figures for three widely separated years suggest that for much of the century nobles owned a greater portion of the debt than non-nobles (see table 10). Between 1608 and 1680 the total number of *pensions* rose by 181 percent while the total amount of capital invested fluctuated, dropping by almost 33 percent at mid-century and rising slightly beyond its earlier level in 1680. More important is the shift in the proportion of capital invested by nobles relative to that invested by non-nobles. Although at no point did the absolute number of nobles owning *pensions* exceed that of non-nobles, the actual amount of capital invested by nobles went from one-third of the total in 1608

---

13. The classic study of civic humanism and the new humanist emphasis on the active life is Hans Baron, *The Crisis of the Early Italian Renaissance: Civic Humanism and Republican Liberty in an Age of Classicism and Tyranny* (Rev. ed.; Princeton, 1966).

14. Robert Harding, *Anatomy of a Power Elite: The Provincial Governors of Early Modern France* (New Haven, 1978), 141; Kettering, *Judicial Politics*, 234.

TABLE 10

Noble and Non-noble Investment in Local Pensions

	1608	1645	1680
Pensions held by nobles	55	75	157
	(44%)	(47%)	(44%)
Pensions held by non-nobles	71	83	197
	(56%)	(53%)	(56%)
Total *pensions*	126	158	354
	(100%)	(100%)	(100%)
Capital from nobles*	329,928	441,549	684,068
	(33%)	(65%)	(57%)
Capital from non-nobles*	679,428	237,520	514,993
	(67%)	(35%)	(43%)
Total capital invested*	1,009,356	679,069	1,199,061
	(100%)	(100%)	(100%)
Mean noble investment*	5,999	5,887	4,357
Mean non-noble investment*	9,569	2,862	2,614

*In livres-tournois.
Source: AC, Aix, CC274, CC277, CC285, "Dettes de la ville."

to substantial majorities of it in the later years. In 1680 the mean holding of nobles who invested in *pensions* was two-thirds greater than that of non-nobles—exactly reversing the situation that had existed in 1608. That early difference was due in part to bourgeois investors whose *pensions* were so large that they skewed the average—one individual, for example, owned a *pension* worth more than 32,000 livres. By mid-century that kind of large-scale roturier investment was gone and noble investment had increased significantly, so that the nobility was clearly funding the major portion of the public debt.

The foregoing discussion, like table 10 itself, is based on *all* noble investment in the municipal debt, including the *pensions* of nobles who were not part of the native nobility. When the *pensions* of the Aixois are isolated from those of the larger nobility residing and investing in Aix, and when the native-noble investments are further broken down to compare old families and new families, some rather striking subpatterns emerge (see table 11). In 1608 investments by Aixois nobles, both old and new, in their town's municipal debt represented only 12 percent of the total noble capital so invested. By

TABLE 11

Native and Non-native Noble Investment in Local Pensions

	1608	1645	1680
Pensions held by native old families	10	20	53
Pensions held by native new families	17	11	34
Total native *pensions*	27	31	87
Investment, native old families*	28,068	94,774	245,671
	(74%)	(61%)	(65%)
Investment, native new families*	10,008	59,840	133,910
	(26%)	(39%)	(35%)
Total native investment*	38,076	154,614	379,581
	(100%)	(100%)	(100%)
Native investment*	38,076	154,614	379,581
	(12%)	(35%)	(56%)
Non-native investment*	291,852	286,935	304,487
	(88%)	(65%)	(44%)
Total noble investment*	329,928	441,549	684,068
	(100%)	(100%)	(100%)

*In livres-tournois.
Source: Same as for table 10.

1645 the native investment in *pensions* had risen to 35 percent of the total, and by 1680 to 56 percent. This dramatic increase involved old noble families and anoblis alike. Although at each of the three points during the century old families owned much more of the municipal debt, in absolute terms, than did new families, both groups avidly adopted this form of investment as time went by: between 1608 and 1680 the amount invested by the old nobility increased by 775 percent while that of anoblis skyrocketed by 1,228 percent; as for the number of investments, the new families doubled their holdings over the same period, and the old nobles held more than five times as many *pensions* in 1680 than they had owned in 1608.

In general, then, it appears that the nobility as a whole was slower than the non-nobles to recognize in *pensions* a good investment opportunity, and the native nobility was even later in coming to this realization. Once they did, however, they assumed a major role in funding the public debt. By the end of the century, not only was the municipal debt of Aix being funded primarily by aristocrats, but on a per capita basis the old Aixois were the single most important group of investors, their fiscal choices directed by a combination of good business sense, the ethics of civic humanism, and a native distrust of royal government. In shifting to modern forms of investment and wealth, these old native families both helped themselves to retain a prominent role in the life of the municipality and, at the same time, demonstrated a critical ability to adjust to changing economic circumstances.

The nobility's role in the life of the urban community extended beyond domination of the town council and funding of the public debt. Since the Middle Ages, southern nobles had defended their towns against invaders and other external threats, a tradition they carried forward into the seventeenth century through the Bureau of Police and the performance of military services. The Bureau of Police was, in fact, an adjunct of the town council, headed by the three consuls and the assessor who led and controlled debates within that body. Because nobles dominated the consulates, they automatically dominated the bureau. There were, in addition, twelve positions of bureau councillor, which as it happened were increasingly drawn from the membership of the town council. Councillors on the bureau served six at a time, alternating every two weeks.[15]

The social composition of the Bureau of Police resembled that of the town council, with both nobles and non-nobles holding slight majorities at different points in the century (see table 12). The positions of initiative and authority in the bureau, however—the consuls and the assessor—rested primarily with nobles. During the years I sampled, a total of 128 nobles were present on the bureau, exactly half of whom came from native Aixois families, 41 from old houses and 23 from new. Again, each of the five families served, but the Séguirans and the Beaumonts appear on the rolls more frequently than any of the others, a fact easily explained by the parallels in membership between the town council and the bureau.

Responsibility for executing the decisions of the bureau belonged to the captains of the five quarters, most of whom appear to have been nobles. Of 65 captains recorded in the records of the town council, 43 were noblemen. They included 21 captains drawn from

15. Gérard Sautel, *Le Bureau de Police d'Aix-en-Provence: Une jurisdiction municipal de police sous l'Ancien Régime* (Paris, 1946), 32–34.

TABLE 12

Social Composition of the Bureau of Police, 1600–1695

	Nobles	Non-nobles	Totals
1600	16 (67%)	8 (33%)	24
1605	6 (46%)	7 (54%)	13
1610	10 (50%)	10 (50%)	20
1615	7 (64%)	4 (36%)	11
1620 (missing)			
1625	8 (42%)	11 (48%)	19
1630	7 (58%)	5 (42%)	12
1635	5 (28%)	13 (72%)	18
1640	6 (55%)	5 (45%)	11
1645	4 (50%)	4 (50%)	8
1650	9 (64%)	5 (36%)	14
1655	9 (56%)	7 (44%)	16
1660	6 (50%)	6 (50%)	12
1665 (missing)			
1670	2 (15%)	11 (85%)	13
1675	8 (73%)	3 (27%)	11
1680	5 (50%)	5 (50%)	10
1685	4 (33%)	8 (67%)	12
1690	4 (36%)	7 (64%)	11
1695	12 (60%)	8 (40%)	20

Source: AC, Aix, Bureau of Police, FF12–62, 1599–1688. I sampled these records by using the names of the councillors present at the first meeting in December every fifth year.

Aixois families (7 old and 14 new).[16] In times of military emergency the captains fulfilled the traditional function of nobility by recruiting and commanding militialike units, usually made up of bourgeois citizens; in peacetime they were responsible for the often unpleasant task of policing their neighborhoods.[17] Here is evidence that nobles did not limit their civic activities to the upper reaches of local government, but regularly participated in the grimy business of seventeenth-century urban life.

In 1628 and 1629 the plague struck southeastern France. News of

16. AC, Aix, BB99-105, "Délibérations du Conseil." Again, I sampled these records by using the minutes of the first meeting for every fifth year during the century. The captains of the various quarters were recorded in these minutes, although less consistently in the first three decades of the period. These numbers are therefore not complete and are offered merely as a sample.

17. Sautel, *Le Bureau de Police,* 46.

the outbreak reached Aix in advance, and the city fathers took des-
perate precautions to prevent infected persons from entering the
town. They stationed guards at all entrances; unfortunately, two soldiers admitted a woman whose symptoms they had mistakenly diag-
nosed as a simple tumor. Within a few days plague had appeared in
each of the five quarters, and officials were forced to take more dras-
tic action to combat its spread.[18] The town council created a special
agency, the Bureau of Health, to monitor the progress of the con-
tagion, to supervise the disposal of bodies and other hygienic measures, and to restrict traffic to and from the town. The bureau included the three consuls, various officers from the Parlement,
deputies from each quarter, and some local physicians. With the exception of the physicians, all were noblemen. The meeting of September 20, 1628, for instance, convened with seventeen men present,
fourteen nobles and three doctors (eleven of the nobles were from
native families). At this same session the bureau assigned fourteen
residents the task of controlling the entrances to each quarter.[19]
Eleven of these so-called intendants were nobles, including two
members of the Beaumont family.

Several other members of the five families served during the brief
tenure of the Bureau of Health. As second consul, M. de Beaumont
sat on the bureau during the worst period of the plague, and a relative assumed the position of deputy to the quartier des Cordeliers.
M. le President de Coriolis chaired several sessions of the bureau,
and the name Guiran also appears in the minutes of one meeting.[20]
Although the bureau lasted only the duration of the epidemic, it il-
lustrates one of the less political aspects of the nobility's participation
in the community. Each quarter relied on its noble families for leadership in times of crisis and for attendance to the problems of defense
and the enforcement of local ordinances. Participation in the daily life
of their quarters offered nobles very little reward and certainly no
glory and therefore can be explained only in terms of their own sense
of civic duty, if not the modern concept of noblesse oblige.

The nobles' growing social conscience ultimately took them into

18. Pierre-Joseph de Haitze, *Histoire de la ville d'Aix, capitale de la Provence* (6 vols.;
Aix, 1889), IV, 147–48.

19. ADBR, Aix, B3719, "Bureau de la Santé, 6 Septembre 1628–20 Octobre
1629."

20. *Ibid.*

the realm of urban poor relief, their charitable impulse emerging during the seventeenth century under the influence of several forces and because of the changing nature of charity itself. The image of the French aristocracy was shifting from a medieval one of nobility based on valor to a modern one of nobility based on birth and culture, a change that Schalk attributes to a noble *prise de conscience* caused by excesses during the Wars of Religion and by a general loss of virtue. How was true nobility to be regained? Schalk maintains that the remedy proposed at the time relied on education and culture, and hence on a "modern" definition of aristocracy.[21] An attitude of concern for those less fortunate than oneself might have been another way in which to regain lost virtue or to attain reennoblement. The humanists had, in fact, suggested that civic involvement could produce good or "noble" men (Chapter VII will reveal the extent to which nobles in Aix read and valued that advice).[22] Charity was simply civic humanism in another phase, one that not only ennobled, but that also served as a modern marque de noblesse. In fact, charity was part of the modern concept of noblesse oblige. As additional reinforcement of its value, charity still retained its Christian qualities. In fact, the post-Tridentine Church exhibited a renewed interest in charity, an interest communicated to residents in Aix through the Company of the Holy Sacrament. The Company, a secret confraternity founded in Paris in 1627, had as its purpose good works on a rather grand scale. The brothers worked clandestinely to eliminate begging and heresy through an elaborate network of fifty-six daughter houses that extended their influence to remote places such as Aix.[23]

Civic humanism, the Counter-Reformation, and changes in the accepted images of aristocracy combined to create in the local Aixois

21. Schalk, *From Valor to Pedigree,* Pt. 2.

22. Schalk argues that the humanist influences of the sixteenth century were not responsible for this change in attitudes or image. Although Castiglione accepted birth as the basis of nobility, and virtue as a quality that may or may not accompany nobility, Schalk claims that *The Courtier* was not read extensively in France until the early seventeenth century, when French views of nobility had already come to resemble those of the humanists (*ibid.,* Chap. 3). I maintain that the humanists' influence was still profound, even if delayed, and that the accumulation of humanist writings in the libraries of noble families suggests this (see Chap. VII).

23. Fairchilds, *Poverty and Charity in Aix,* 40–41; Kathryn Norberg, *Rich and Poor in Grenoble, 1600–1814* (Berkeley, 1985), 27–28. In chap. 3, Norberg provides an excellent description of the Company of the Holy Sacrament and its role in helping the poor.

elite a sense of mission with regard to those less fortunate. But the involvement of the nobility in this area, previously the preserve of the Church, also reflects a changing view of charity itself. The unprecedented poverty and misery of the seventeenth century prompted the crown to express an interest in charity, particularly during the reign of Louis XIV. The inevitable lack of resources—and a certain lack of initiative—meant that the king tended to rely on private institutions rather than on his own bureaucracy. Instead of creating its own system for public assistance, royal government merely encouraged the development of private facilities, or *hôpitaux*. Cissie Fairchilds describes the privately run hospitals as a critical transitional phase between almsgiving and public assistance.[24]

Residents of Aix had witnessed outbreaks of incredible misery, triggered by the plague and by recurrent poor harvests, that left crowds of destitute and homeless beggars a feature of everyday life. Fairchilds reports that during the Revolt of the Cascaveoux in 1630, starving agricultural laborers streamed into the town, where they joined artisans in three days of riots and pillage, most of which was directed toward the wealthy.[25] Events such as this, needless to say, alerted local notables to the necessity of poor relief. In Aix as elsewhere, as the result of private rather than royal initiative, the century saw the foundation of numerous hospitals, which acted as middlemen and gradually claimed the responsibility of dispensing food and medical assistance to the poor.[26]

The transfer of charity from the hands of the Church to institutional hands also made possible the surveillance of the down and out, particularly with regard to their moral condition. Inevitably during this period of economic stagnation, unemployment, and vagrancy, the idea took hold that poverty and idleness lead to crime and sin. After all, the citizens of Aix had been regularly subjected to the vagaries and violence of the poor. Ideally, the institutionalization of charity had the underlying purpose of eliminating a breeding ground for crime—poverty; more realistically, it served to confine the poor. Hospitals could put the idle to work, or at least contain them, and

24. Fairchilds, *Poverty and Charity in Aix,* 23, 37.

25. *Ibid.,* 23. See also René Pillorget, "Un document concernant la peste et l'insurrection d'Aix (1630)," *Revue de la Méditerranée,* XXI (1961), 209–21.

26. Fairchilds, *Poverty and Charity in Aix,* 27.

thus reduce a potential threat to the welfare of local residents. In this way charity became a matter of civic importance rather than just a matter of good works, and as such it drew heavily upon the support of the local nobility.[27]

Administrative responsibility for the hospitals, as with the Bureau of Health, rested primarily with nobles, who exercised control through boards of rectors. Diefendorf found that in sixteenth-century Paris the families that assumed the most responsibility for charitable and lay religious institutions were those that were most active in municipal politics. The same was true of Aix, where boards of rectors came to be overwhelmingly aristocratic in composition. The rectors met twice a week, and shared in turn the rotating position of *semainier* and other supervisory duties. The *semainier* assumed the daily tasks of overseeing a hospital. He inspected the house, tended to accounts, purchased supplies, and chaired meetings of the board. For this reason the position of rector was usually time-consuming—not to mention expensive, for rectors were expected to donate generously to their hospitals and at times were liable for their debts. Early in the century the bourgeoisie tended to dominate the boards of various hospitals, but in the 1620s nobles began to offer their time and services. By the middle of the century, the nobility controlled most of the boards and thus the administration of most charities in Aix, seats on the boards often being passed from one generation to the next. (Fairchilds attributes the shift in composition from bourgeois to noble to the fact that the Company of the Holy Sacrament made charity a very fashionable activity for noblemen and noblewomen.) At the same time, the staffs of hospitals welcomed the prestige of having nobles and senior parlementaires on their administrative boards. And finally, the nobility had come to recognize in charity a tremendous service to the community of Aix, as "their primary concern was for a moral policing of the poor" in the community's interest.[28]

Hôpital Saint-Jacques, founded in 1519, was the oldest and one of the most important institutions of its kind in Aix. It was conceived to provide medical assistance to the indigent, but it excluded victims of

27. *Ibid.*, 24–33; Nicole Sabaratier, *L'Hôpital Saint-Jacques d'Aix-en-Provence, 1519–1789* (3 vols.; Aix, Thèse de droit, 1964), I, 16–18.

28. Diefendorf, *Paris City Councillors*, 71; Fairchilds, *Poverty and Charity in Aix*, 40–43, 37.

venereal diseases, leprosy, smallpox, the plague, and insanity. By the seventeenth century the rectors of Saint-Jacques were mostly noble. A sampling at five-year intervals from 1610 to 1690 shows that the board's membership was never less than 64 percent noble, and usually far more. Sometimes the entire board—which had anywhere from seven to fifteen members—was made up of noblemen.[29] During those years eighty-nine positions were held by members of the native nobility, forty-seven by persons from old families and forty-two by anoblis. The five families donated their time generously to Saint-Jacques, particularly the two old families: the Guirans sat on its board at least sixteen years during the century, and the Coriolis twelve years. The three new families served less often: the Beaumonts seven years, the Séguirans six years, and the Mazargues only one year.

Hôpital de la Charité was established in 1640 as a refuge for orphans, the elderly, and the jobless. La Charité also aided unemployed residents in their homes by distributing bread when they were in need. By the late seventeenth century the hospital was routinely dispensing about 4,000 loaves of bread, or *secours à domicile,* to about 410 destitute people a week. Like Saint-Jacques, La Charité was administered largely by nobles; fourteen of its eighteen rectors in 1680 were noble.[30]

Along with Saint-Jacques and La Charité, Aix boasted twenty-one other charitable institutions that tended to the various needs of the poor and the ill. Fairchilds reports that fifteen different facilities were created in the seventeenth century alone. Among the things provided were a home for reformed prostitutes, a charity to ransom Christian slaves taken by the Turks, a charity for the dowries of poor orphan girls, various orphanages, and several hospitals for the disabled or the "incurables." Because of the number of its charities, Aix was described in the seventeenth century as a "ville hospitalière." Its charities were "uniquely municipal institutions, objects of civic pride to the town as a whole."[31] The nobility, given the extent of their involvement in their urban community, naturally assumed leadership

29. Sabaratier, *L'Hôpital Saint-Jacques,* I, 72; ADBR, Aix, XXH-E3 to XXH-E6, Hôpital Saint-Jacques, "Registre des grands bureaux depuis 1602 jusques à 1636."
30. Fairchilds, *Poverty and Charity in Aix,* 21, 94–95, ADBR, Aix, XXIH-E20, Hôpital de la Charité, "Délibérations du Bureau Général, 1662–1760."
31. Fairchilds, *Poverty and Charity in Aix,* 19–20, 16.

of this aspect of town life too. Most of the Aixois who became involved in these charitable efforts belonged to families that, like the Coriolis, were deeply entrenched in provincial and municipal government.[32] Very often the rectors of charities were themselves officers in the Parlement or the Cour des Comptes, and there appears to have been a strong relationship between officeholding, political activity, and philanthropy.

Nobles also shouldered much of the financial burden for the charities. Their contributions took various forms—testamentary bequests, *pensions, dons gratuits*—and their reasons for giving undoubtedly varied as well. Certainly, the fate of their souls still moved some nobles to donate. In fact, Aix was inundated in the seventeenth century by pamphlets in which authors promised that God would look kindly upon generous souls. But considerations other than fear of purgatory also prompted contributions; altruism and noblesse oblige must have inspired many. In studying the wills of all social groups in eighteenth-century Aix, Michel Vovelle found that 70 percent of them listed gifts to local hospitals, a fact he attributes to the valuable example set by the local nobility.[33]

Whether it was concern for the community or concern for their own salvation that inspired these aristocrats to philanthropy, their donations were an important source of revenue for charities. Among the sixty-eight testators of the five families, forty-two made bequests to charities, confraternities, churches or religious orders, or some combination of these. Eleven of the forty-two gave solely to churches or convents; thirty-one gave money directly to hospitals or to confraternities associated with various charities in addition to making gifts to the Church. Although the figures for direct contribution fall short of those mentioned by Vovelle for the eighteenth century, they are nevertheless impressive because charity in an institutionalized form was relatively new to Aix in the seventeenth century, and many Aixois still preferred to channel their contributions to the poor through the established agency of the Church, often specifying the number of masses they hoped would be said in their memory.

The five families gave most frequently to Saint-Jacques, La Misé-

32. The Guirans served on the board of La Charité seven years; the Coriolis three; the Séguirans four; the Beaumonts one; and the Mazargues five.

33. Fairchilds, *Poverty and Charity in Aix,* 55–56; Michel Vovelle, *Piété baroque et déchristianisation en Provence au XVIIIe siècle* (Paris, 1973), 246.

ricorde, and La Charité, the three largest hospitals in Aix. Their legacies were not always in money. Sextius de Séguiran, writing his will
in 1679, left 1,200 livres to various hospitals and requested that when
he died all the wheat on his property be harvested and distributed
among those in need. Similarly, Jean-Baptiste de Mazargues left 600
livres and one charge of wheat to La Charité. On occasion, nobles
named specific charities as universal heirs to their estates, as in the
case of Jean de Coriolis, who left three-fourths of his property to La
Charité and one-fourth to the Oeuvre de la Rédemption des Captifs.
In 1692 Françoise de Beaumont wrote a will in which she gave an
annual *pension* to her brother, 1,500 livres to her nephew, some property to her two servants, and the remainder of her estate to Saint-
Jacques and La Miséricorde. After medical and funeral expenses were
deducted, her legacy to Saint-Jacques alone consisted of 3,680 livres,
nine quintaux of olive oil, and a five-piece Bergamot tapestry.[34] Testamentary bequests such as these again point to the change in attitudes about charity that accompanied the rise of hospitals in the seventeenth-century. Charity retained its religious properties, but it had
definitely acquired a civic importance as well. That nobles dominated the administration and donated freely to the endowment of
charity was simply another aspect of the aristocracy's role in town
life, one that involved the relatively modern notion of obligations on
the part of those who enjoy privileges by birth.

34. ADBR, Aix, Fonds Berlie, 301E-296, 1679, pp. 22–27; Fonds Bertrand,
302E-1179, 1651–53, pp. 769–78; Fonds Mouravit, 307E-963, 1663, pp. 636–41;
Fonds Laucagne, 306E-937, 1691–92, pp. 658–61; XXH-B64, Hôpital Saint-Jacques,
"Legs Beaumont."

VI

PROVINCIAL POLITICS
AND WARFARE

In previous chapters I have reiterated the distinctive qualities imparted to the Aixois nobility by its urban location and its participation in municipal government and civic affairs. Unquestionably, the nobility controlled the town; Aix in turn served the nobility as a power base in the larger arena of provincial government and politics. In their commitment to matters and institutions that concerned Provence at large, however, the Aixois exhibited a trait common to most provincial nobilities: throughout France provincial politics, like military commissions and tax exemptions, identified nobility as a privileged elite. To the extent that they engaged in politics and warfare, nobles in Aix conformed to the traditional image of the French nobility. To the extent that their political activity reflected their urban power base, they were, of course, more unusual. The political implications of their participation in the government and politics of the province are very important. The first half of the seventeenth century saw the city of Aix engulfed in a bitter struggle to prevent any further extension of royal authority in Provence; the second half witnessed a cooperative effort between local nobles and that same central authority, a development that was mutually beneficial because it both accommodated the state-building programs of Louis XIV and promoted the political power of factions within the local urban nobility.

The period of Cardinal Richelieu and Cardinal Mazarin was one of recurring political crises and rebellion in Provence as elsewhere. Specifically, the institutional reforms of the period touched off a series of revolts in which the nobility of Aix played a highly visible role. On the whole their reactions to reform were guided by the clienteles to which they belonged, clienteles that infiltrated all the political theaters of the conflict. They included the Estates of Provence, the positions of the procureurs du pays, the Assembly of the Nobility, and the Parlement. Each of these institutions was dominated by factions of nobles in which the Aixois were well represented and exercised considerable influence; as procureurs du pays and as the largest local group in the Parlement, the Aixois had their greatest impact on provincial affairs.

A *pays d'état,* Provence traditionally benefited from the protection of representative assemblies against royal attacks on provincial privileges. The fiery Provençaux particularly treasured the right of their Estates to approve, collect, and apportion taxes—a regional prerogative that acted as a check on royal authority. The composition of the Estates of Provence included deputies of the first estate (the clergy); the second estate (all fiefholding noblemen); and the third estate (deputies from the chief town in each viguerie of Provence). The nobility, with about 150 members, was the largest of the three orders, and since voting was conducted by head rather than by order, the second estate enjoyed an important numerical advantage.[1] The provincial governor called annual meetings of the Estates to debate and to apportion taxes, the most important of which was the taille réelle. After assessment, local responsibility for collection of taxes fell on viguerie officials who received monies from taxpayers and transferred them to the provincial treasurer; he in turn channeled these funds to the trésoriers généraux de France.[2]

Between sessions of the Estates, the procureurs du pays tended to all administrative matters. By the late sixteenth century it was customary for the archbishop of Aix, the three consuls of Aix, and the assessor of Aix to hold the positions of *procureurs du pays nés.* In addition, each estate was represented on this committee by two *procureurs joints.* Since the procureurs du pays were charged during interim periods with safeguarding provincial interests—often in opposition to

1. Major, *Representative Government,* 89–90; Jonathan L. Pearl, *Guise and Provence: Political Conflict in the Epoch of Richelieu,* Microfilm (Ann Arbor, 1968), 49–51. For a detailed explanation of the way in which the composition of the Estates evolved, see Gaspard H. Coriolis, *Dissertation sur les Etats de Provence* (Aix, 1867), 11–101.

2. Kettering, *Judicial Politics,* 58–59; Major, *Representative Government,* 90.

the crown—their responsibilities were considerable. They acted as a sort of grievance committee, "taking their complaints right to the throne."[3] At the same time the procureurs enforced ordinances passed by the Estates, a duty that saw their intervention in and supervision over many provincial matters. The procureurs nés dealt with the daily problems of executing decisions of the Estates. Meetings of the procureurs nés et joints, however, were called between sessions of the Estates to address new issues.[4]

As the executive committee of the Estates, the procureurs had an important role in tax administration, including the right to examine the books of the provincial treasurers before they were turned over to the Chambre des Comptes for audit. The procureurs directed construction and maintenance of all highways and bridges in Provence, and their jurisdiction also included such problems as public health and the billeting of troops. The bulk of correspondence from Louis XIII and Louis XIV to the procureurs concerned, in fact, the costs and logistics of housing and feeding royal troops in the region, as well as the maintenance of local fortifications.[5]

Faced with the growing financial burden of the Wars of Religion, the governors of Provence were forced in the sixteenth century to seek additional taxes to pay the salaries of troops. Because the procureurs du pays did not have the authority to impose taxes without the approval of a representative body, and because the Estates regularly refused to approve new taxes, the provincial governors sought the alternative of calling deputies from various communities together when the Estates were not in session. This Assembly of Communities consisted of the procureurs nés et joints and deputies from nineteen communities in Provence. The Assembly of Communities and the Estates were separate bodies, but their functions were not specifically delineated. Often the assembly was called to deal with

3. Major, *Representative Government*, 91; Pearl, *Guise and Provence*, 96; Bruno Durand, "Le Rôle des consuls d'Aix dans l'administration du pays," *Provence historique*, VI (1956), 252.

4. Coriolis, *Dissertation sur les Etats de Provence*, 122.

5. Kettering, *Judicial Politics*, 59; Major, *Representative Government*, 91; Durand, "Le Rôle des consuls d'Aix," 254–57; A. Bourde, "La Provence au grand siècle," in *Histoire de Provence*, ed. Edouard Baratier (Toulouse, 1969), 312; Louis Blancard, ed., *Inventaire sommaire des archives départementales des Bouches-du-Rhône*, Ser. C (Marseille, 1884–92), II, 1–3.

the same issues that the Estates would have addressed had it been in session.[6]

Within a short span of time royal officials began to display an obvious preference for the Assembly of Communities over the Estates. For one reason, the assembly could be convoked more rapidly because preliminary viguerie meetings to elect deputies were not necessary. More important, the Estates was more costly to hold and frequently impossible to manage. Moreover, the assembly, whose membership and voting procedure were not weighted in favor of the usually contentious Provençal nobles, tended to grant most of the requested taxes. By the end of the sixteenth century, royal government clearly preferred to deal with the Assembly of Communities, and after 1639 the Estates never met again.[7]

Whether working with the Estates or the assembly, the offices of procureurs du pays were central in the administration of the province. And as the procureurs nés, the consuls and the assessor of Aix were cardinal figures in the system, this in addition to their local roles as the executive branch of municipal government in Aix. The vast majority (77 percent) of the consuls and assessors in the seventeenth century were nobles, and 137 (46 percent) of these were natives of Aix. Thus, by virtue of their municipal positions, the Aixois were central to the administration of the province as well.[8]

It was not only by serving as procureurs du pays that nobles in Aix participated in provincial political issues; they also figured prominently in another important institution, the General Assembly of the Nobility of Provence. This forum debated all matters that pertained to the nobility, particularly the defense of traditional privileges such as the tax-exempt status of fiefs. Out of self-interest, the Assembly frequently found itself averse to the desires of royal government. In 1639, for example, the war with the Hapsburgs forced the crown to call the *ban* and *arrière-ban* in Provence, thereby provoking massive resistance from the Provençal aristocracy, who ultimately refused to leave Provence for the battlefield. Subsequently, the Assembly of the Nobility was suspended; it met only three times during the remain-

6. BDR, III, 475–77; Major, *Representative Government,* 92.

7. Major, *Representative Government,* 92; BDR, III, 477.

8. See table 9, p. 00.

ing sixty years of the century, having being replaced by a smaller, less fractious committee of nobles.[9]

During the long intervals that passed between convocations of the Assembly of Nobility, syndics conducted routine business and acted as spokesmen. Customarily, at least one syndic was trained as an attorney and could deal with litigation involving the assembly. Again, the nobles of Aix served regularly as syndics during the seventeenth century; the list includes the names of Honoré, Pierre, and Joseph Coriolis. Between 1598 and 1700, the Assembly of the Nobility had a total of 133 syndics, 37 of whom were native to Aix, a figure that represents 28 percent of all the syndics and that suggests once again the extent to which the Aixois were involved in the affairs of the provincial nobility. Furthermore, the Aixois routinely served as *commissaires* of the nobility. These were nobles elected by the assembly to guard and control membership by investigating the noble status of those who joined. Of 83 commissaires during the seventeenth century, 36 (or 43 percent) were Aixois.[10] They included four members of the Coriolis family and one Séguiran. Acting in this capacity, the Aixois were not only prominent within the Assembly of the Nobility, but were able to control and shape its membership as well. This control necessarily afforded them tremendous power within the greater Provençal nobility.

For all these reasons the protagonists of early seventeenth-century disputes with royal agents were often noble residents of Aix. Indeed, Laurant de Coriolis instigated one of the most serious of these incidents, the one that developed into the open insurrection known as the Revolt of the Cascaveoux. The revolt occurred in 1630 as a response to the creation of élections in Provence. In 1629 a royal edict called for the establishment of ten élections and 350 positions of *élus* to assess and collect the taille, a responsibility traditionally claimed by the Estates of Provence. Meanwhile, Richelieu raised the salt tax, the *taillon* (a tax supplemental to the taille and generally raised to meet military emergencies), and the *don gratuit* (here the term refers

9. EDB, III, 508–14.

10. B. Méjanes, Aix, MS 1144 (1074) "Etat chronologique et héraldique des messires les syndics du corps de la noblesse de Provence. . . ."; Mousnier, *Institutions of France,* I, 200; B. Méjanes, MS 1144 (1074) "Etat chronologique et héraldique des messires les commissaires du corps de la noblesse de Provence. . . ."

to a lump-sum "contribution" to the crown levied in the south on a province as a whole). The independent-minded Provençaux correctly regarded these actions, together with the proposed élus, as infringements on their traditional rights and as an effort to supplant their Estates. Contributing to their long-standing animosity toward the crown was the fact that Richelieu had also increased troop movements in the area to support his campaign against Protestants in neighboring Languedoc and to assist with the war in Italy. Moreover, the cardinal demanded of the Provençaux seven hundred mules and muleteers, an imposition that placed great financial strain on the resources of several communities. On top of that, in order to provide for his troops, Richelieu prohibited the export of grain from the province. Faced with the élus, with tax increases and other unpopular fiscal measures, and with the unpleasantness of troops billeted upon them, the Estates of Provence demanded that the king revoke all the edicts in question. Their requests were, of course, denied.[11]

Discontent with the crown was therefore rife in Provence when the plague appeared in June, 1629, indirectly igniting an already volatile and miserable situation. Predictably, the plague arrived on the heels of a major subsistence crisis in Provence, one that was exacerbated by the destruction done by Richelieu's troops and the demands they placed on a declining supply of wheat, oats, and other grains, with the result that the price of wheat climbed steadily from 1625 to 1630 (see graph 1, p. 30). The growing scarcity and rising cost of bread combined with the outbreak of plague in the fall of 1629 to heighten tension and anxieties among residents of Aix. The plague was also responsible for the fateful decision to divide the Parlement.[12]

To escape the epidemic, the Parlement voted to leave Aix and to adjourn in two separate groups to the uninfected towns of Salon and

11. Major, *Representative Government*, 542–44; Pearl, *Guise and Provence*, 184–97; Kettering, *Judicial Politics*, 54–64; René Pillorget, *Les mouvements insurrectionnels*, 314–20; Pillorget, "The *Cascaveoux*: The Insurrection at Aix of Autumn of 1630," in *State and Society in Seventeenth-Century France*, ed. Raymond Kierstead (New York, 1975), 96–97. Finally, Peiresc commented in 1629, in one of his letters to Monsieur Dupuy, on the destruction caused by the troop movements. See Nicolas Claude Fabri de Peiresc, *Lettres aux frères Dupuy*, ed. Philippe Tamizey de Larroque (7 vols.; Paris, 1890), II, 46–47.

12. Pillorget, *Les mouvements insurrectionnels*, 314–15; "The *Cascaveoux*," 98–99.

Pertuis, there being no single uncontaminated town in Provence large enough to support the entire court. The group of parlementaires that arrived in Salon was under the leadership of First President Vincent-Anne de Forbin-Maynier d'Oppède, a client of Richelieu; the other magistrates followed Laurant de Coriolis, second president and Baron de Corbières, to the town of Pertuis. This separation of the parlementaires worsened factional rivalry and created a major power struggle within the court, as was confirmed on March 20, 1630, when Coriolis entered the chamber at Pertuis wearing the vestments of the first president, an act that seemed to symbolize the sovereignty of this Parlement. Naturally, his actions distressed and provoked Oppède, who immediately gained from Paris orders to reunite the two courts. Suspicious of the first president, Coriolis and his court resisted until September, after which both Parlements finally rejoined in Aix.[13]

Although the two groups of magistrates were now seated together, the division between them persisted, and disputes regularly interrupted subsequent proceedings. Coriolis, supported by a host of clients and sympathizers, demanded the position of first president as retribution for the poor treatment suffered by the parlementaires in Pertuis, and to this end he and his clients used the arrival of the intendant, Dreux d'Aubray, as an excuse to set off a popular revolt in late September. Aubray had traveled to Aix with the purpose of registering the royal edict that would establish the élus in Provence. Here he encountered the Revolt of the Cascaveoux, unquestionably instigated by Coriolis, who, a contemporary writes, encouraged citizens to arm themselves, even proclaiming that "we must kill those who wish to establish the élus."[14]

Both Aubray and Oppède were forced to flee Aix after a mob attacked their hôtels, leaving Coriolis in control of the Parlement. On October 18, the Parlement refused to register the royal edict and for-

13. Kettering, *Judicial Politics*, 156–57; Kettering, *Patrons, Brokers, and Clients*, 159, 190.

14. Kettering, *Judicial Politics*, 156–157; Pearl, *Guise and Provence*, 199–200. In Provençal the word for "bell" is *cascaveou*. The revolt is so named because of a classical allusion made during a public speech by Paul de Joannis, a nephew of Coriolis, who proclaimed that he himself would bell the cat, Aubray, for self-protection. Thenceforth the rebels were known by the small bells they wore attached to their coats. Kettering, *Judicial Politics*, 159.

bade citizens to accept positions as élus. Meanwhile, the Estates convened in Aix and pronounced its support for the parlementaires by sending a deputation to the king to demand the revocation of the edict. The Estates also requisitioned funds to purchase additional guns and munitions for other communities to use in defense of their provincial liberties. Aix, however, remained the focus of the rebellion, its nobility acting as the primary catalyst. A Parisian visitor to Aix during the turmoil wrote that the local nobility "had rendered these élus so detestable and so horrible to the populace, that they had formed an opposition party, named the *cascaveu*. . . . They were resolved to close the gates to the king himself, they said, if he came in order to establish the élus."[15]

But the previously united front against Oppède and the crown began to disintegrate in early November. On November 3 and 4, circumstances became uncontrollable and the residents of Aix experienced a night of rioting and terror as marauding peasants pillaged the Place des Prêcheurs. These events resulted in the formation of an opposition party, the "Blue Ribbon." Headed by the first consul, the baron de Bras, the group deplored and condemned Coriolis' machinations and his self-serving use of the mob in Aix. René Pillorget describes the events that ensued as a factional struggle for control of Aix, instigated at least in part by a fear of the populace. Many notables of Aix had been frightened by Coriolis' success in mobilizing their social inferiors; threatened by these unconstrained popular forces, they began to resist the Cascaveoux.[16] This opposing faction, however, still posed as defenders of provincial liberties, while at the same time expressing their loyalty to the king. By the end of November, what had begun as a defense of provincial liberties and a power struggle within the Parlement had become a major factional struggle, complete with a dimension of social or class conflict, for control of the city.

In early December, Baron de Bras successfully engineered Coriolis' expulsion from the city along with those of Coriolis' nephew and cohort Paul de Joannis and several other supporters. The movement's

<hr />

15. Major, *Representative Government,* 547–48; Pearl, *Guise and Provence,* 200–204. The quotation is Pearl's translation (p. 204) of remarks made by Jean Jacques Bouchard in *Son Voyage de Paris à Rome en 1630* (Paris, 1881), 114.

16. Pillorget, "The *Cascaveoux,*" 111–12.

strength appeared to be rapidly deteriorating.[17] But the continuing threat of violence from Coriolis' proletarian supporters and dismay at the treatment served someone of Coriolis' rank and stature induced Parlement to recall him to Aix and to permit him to continue as a president. Moreover, the first consul had meanwhile discredited himself by provoking a brawl between his supporters and a captain of a quarter who refused to execute one of his orders. The Parlement attempted to mediate this dispute but in the end resorted to assisting the first consul and some supporters in safely fleeing the city.[18] This retreat appeared to leave the Cascaveoux in control of Aix once again.

Coriolis did not stop there, however. His partisans produced a polemic, entitled "Laophile," that portrayed him as "the father of the people," and the Blue Ribbon as "seditious enemies of the king." It also maintained that the Coriolis machine enjoyed the support of Marie de Médicis—but notables soon learned that the queen mother's support was of no consequence: on December 12 the duke of Guise informed Aix about the famous Day of the Dupes, in which against all expectations the king suddenly had turned against his mother and Michel de Marillac, the keeper of the seals, siding instead with Richelieu; it was instantly apparent that Coriolis could not count on Marie or her agents for assistance. Furthermore, Richelieu had dispatched the prince of Condé and 5,000 troops, along with two intendants, to restore order in Provence. The always-pragmatic cardinal had abandoned Marillac's absolutist policies and had authorized the prince instead to appease the Provençaux.[19]

With appeasement, order, and fiscal urgency in mind, Condé convoked the provincial Estates on March 7 at the town of Tarascon. Here he negotiated a compromise by which the edict on *élections* would be revoked and the Estates would in return consent to 1.5 million livres in taxes to be paid over a period of four years. Having resolved the king's fiscal problems, Condé and his troops then moved on to the city of Aix to reestablish order and to punish the rebels. Overall, Condé acted magnanimously toward the Aixois. Residents temporarily lost their right to elect consuls, and the intendants made

17. *Ibid.*, 115–16; Pearl, *Guise and Provence*, 204–206.
18. Pillorget, "The *Cascaveoux*," 115–16.
19. *Ibid.*, 117; Major, *Representative Government*, 584–86.

the obligatory examples of a few rabble-rousers by sentencing one to death and the others to the galleys. Coriolis and company fled to Les Baux, where they linked up with the duke of Orléans and partici-pated in the Montmorency rebellion. Eventually, Coriolis' luck ran out—he was apprehended and imprisoned.[20]

During the Cascaveoux revolt the Parlement had made little effort to control the violence. At times it actually contributed to the in-surrection by sending remonstrances against the élus to Paris. The court's failure to take repressive measures resulted largely from the fact that the Coriolis network of clients controlled its deliberations. In the absence of Oppède, Coriolis himself presided over sessions of the court, and unusually high rates of absenteeism left him with very little opposition. Thus Coriolis and his supporters could successfully manipulate the Parlement to remonstrate against the élus and to re-main silent while his men fomented rebellion among the populace. His clients numbered fifteen members of Parlement, and he claimed the support of at least five others.[21] The heart of the Revolt of the Cascaveoux was this Coriolis network of noble clients and relatives organized in defense of their provincial rights and seeking retribution for their treatment at Pertuis. Pillorget argues that this insurrection against the king rapidly became a feud among rival factions to con-trol the city and the Parlement. Coriolis' opponents played on fears of a popular movement to alienate notables from the movement and thereby to undermine his aristocratic base of support. According to Pillorget, divisions among notables contributed mightily to the fail-ure of the revolt. Combined with the highly localized nature of the rebellion, this lack of unity permitted the king to extinguish the re-volt militarily, and rather easily.[22] But that did not mean the end of opposition to the fiscal policies of the crown, nor did it mean the end of factional strife within the city.

Nine years later royal agents demanded of the Provençaux an ad-ditional 400,000 livres annually to support troops stationed in the re-gion until the end of the war with the Hapsburgs. The king con-voked the Estates of Provence to approve the request. But the Estates opposed the tax increase, forcing him to turn to the Assembly of

20. Major, *Representative Government*, 587; Pillorget, "The *Cascaveoux*," 121.
21. Kettering, *Judicial Politics*, 175.
22. *Ibid.*, 122–23.

Communities, which complied with most of his wishes. Louis also called the *ban* and *arrière-ban,* but the Assembly of the Nobility ignored the crown's appeal for military and financial assistance. As noted earlier, 1639 saw the final session of the Estates, and the Assembly of the Nobility met only three times after this date.[23]

In addition to installing unpopular fiscal measures, the crown insured the survival of what Kettering has described as an opposition party within the Parlement by attempting to find an immediate remedy to budgetary problems through the creation of numerous new judicial offices. The "opposition" parlementaires vigorously protested the establishment of a Chambre des Requêtes, the offices in which would raise 370,000 livres for the crown. The opposition feared, among other things, that the proliferation of judicial offices would deflate the value of their own sinecures. There were important links between this opposition party and the Cascaveoux; several members had participated in the earlier revolt, and as before, they continued to pursue their own interests in a growing antagonism between the Parlement on the one hand and the crown and the provincial governor on the other.[24]

In the absence of the Estates and the Assembly of the Nobility, elements within the nobility of Aix attempted to obstruct royal policy through the Parlement and the offices of the procureurs du pays. A revolt against the very unpopular provincial governor, the count d'Alais, in 1649 ushered in the period of the Fronde in Provence. The concessions sought by the opposition parlementaires—a party maintained by a network of kinship, clientage, and friendship—reveal a determination to defy unpopular royal edicts. For one, the parlementaires requested the abolition of the Semester, a disciplinary and revenue-producing device with the purpose of controlling the unruly Parlement by first dividing it and then packing it with judges loyal to the crown. This royal contrivance had been instituted by the provincial governor the previous year with no local assent. The Semester was abolished in return for 200,000 livres compensation, and the Chambre des Requêtes for 300,000 livres. The parlementaires also protested the presence of 3,500 soldiers billeted in Aix without the

23. Major, *Representative Government,* 601–602; EDB, III, 514.
24. Kettering, *Judicial Politics,* 191. Kettering describes the opposition party and its reaction to the fiscal policies of Mazarin in Chap. 6 of *Judicial Politics.*

approval of the procureurs (the troops were subsequently removed) and objected vigorously to royal interference with free municipal elections, particularly to the presence of the governor's appointees in elective offices (a royal edict later reconfirmed the elective nature of municipal government in Provençal towns). Altogether the parlementaires presented fifteen grievances to the crown during the course of the revolt, most of which had nothing to do with provincial privileges but instead addressed the threat of new judicial offices and were to protect the parlementaires' own interests as part of a privileged elite. Faced with insurrection, Mazarin agreed to make several changes, although none proved to be of any permanence. After 1650 and this preliminary revolt, the opposition party as such came to an end. Some of its members, the so-called Sabreurs, reassembled on the side of the princes for the civil war that took place in Provence from 1650 to 1653. Others supported Mazarin during the Fronde.[25]

Ultimately, it was the new governor, the duke of Mercoeur, who ended the rebellion by persuading the rebels to join him. Mercoeur was the nephew of Mazarin by marriage, and Mazarin's trust appeared to be well placed in him, for in what Kettering describes as "one of the most spectacular switches in Provençal politics," he secured the services of Henri de Forbin-Maynier d'Oppède. More specifically, Mercoeur secured an alliance with the chiefs of the opposition, Oppède and the baron de Saint-Marc, and their clients followed suit. Since many of the Sabreurs were relatives and clients of Oppède, his decision to switch sides tipped the balance of power and influence in favor of Mercoeur and Cardinal Mazarin. As reward for their affiliation, Saint-Marc was made captain of Mercoeur's guards and Oppède first president of the Parlement. In fact, Oppède had competed for this honor with Charles de Grimaldi, the marquis de Régusse, who after 1649 led the Mazarinistes and who actually insured the loyalty of the Parlement for the cardinal in 1651. Despite his earlier loyalty, Régusse was passed over in favor of Oppède, whose influence and credit in the province were recognized by Mazarin and Mercoeur as much greater.[26]

In short, Oppède had persuaded his new patron that he had suffi-

25. Ibid., 211, 271–77, 285–87.
26. Kettering, Patrons, Brokers, and Clients, 45; Kettering, Judicial Politics, 296.

cient clients to establish royal control in Provence, an actuality amply demonstrated in the municipal elections of 1650–1651, when the baron's men defeated the clients of Régusse. Oppède's clientele would in fact continue to dominate municipal government and the critical positions of consuls during his years as a ministerial client. He attempted to justify his change in allegiance during the Fronde and to reconcile it with provincial welfare by couching it in terms of a family tradition of royal service and by suggesting that his newly acquired influence at court could ultimately benefit the province. There was a certain amount of truth in Oppède's argument: through his working with Mazarin rather than against him he helped to advance royal interests, but not at the expense of provincial institutions such as the Assembly of Communities. This much, at least, was in the interest of Provence, not to mention the fact that peace had been restored.[27]

Oppède's switch contributed to a restoration of order by 1652, but the tension between the Sabreurs and the Mazarinistes persisted during the remainder of the decade. Violence erupted for a third time in 1659, centering around the procureurs du pays, the Parlement, and the clients of Régusse. Renewed fighting in Italy had forced Mazarin to raise taxes and to increase troop movements in Provence. In January, 1658, Governor Mercoeur demanded of locals both quarters and money for his troops. The procureurs refused. The governor and the intendant responded with *lettres de cachet* (warrants) for the first consul of Aix, Forbin de la Barben. Still, the procureurs refused consent. In May, 1658, the intendant for the army, de Chouppes, and Lieutenant General de Marsilly presented lettres de cachet for payment and quarters to the provincial treasurer, Gaillard, and to the first president of the Cour des Comptes, Séguiran, but both were adamant about the necessity of approval by the procureurs. Meanwhile, unpaid soldiers had streamed into Aix, where they provoked confrontations with crowds that had assembled to protest the arrest of the first consul and the imposition of the proposed tax. In May, 1658, Oppède, who was by then acting intendant and whom Kettering describes as "the new instrument of centralization in Provence," announced that the intendant would have the authority to raise the

27. Kettering, *Patrons, Brokers, and Clients*, 47, 64–65.

additional levies without the consent of the procureurs. The procureurs naturally condemned this as an attack on provincial privilege, and the Parlement responded by annulling Oppède's ordinance.[28]

Resentment toward Oppède mounted steadily, even among some parlementaires who had sided with him during the Fronde. Now many saw him as betraying the interests of the Parlement and usurping more and more power within provincial administration. Resentful of Oppède's increasing power and anxious to disqualify his major rival, Régusse was behind much of the opposition and popular protest against the military tax. Oppède had not forgotten the rivalry either; he did his utmost to poison Mazarin's impressions of Régusse, and eventually succeeded. In fact, Régusse was exiled from Aix for one year in 1658, after Oppède and Mercoeur persuaded Mazarin that the marquis was responsible for a popular protest against a new military tax. In Régusse's absence, his clients and supporters continued to cast Oppède as a public enemy, while former Sabreurs usually remained loyal to him.[29]

The uneasy situation deteriorated into open insurrection on Saint Valentine's Day, 1659, when a shooting incident began several days of violence instigated by armed noblemen demanding the arrest of Oppède, whom they believed was responsible. Oppède took refuge in the archbishop's private apartments. There he was held captive for ten days while Aix once again became a battleground for two feuding noble factions. On February 27, Governor Mercoeur entered Aix with troops to quell the revolt. He arrived with 2,000 infantry, 200 cavalry, 80 nobles, and 15 companies of provincial infantry. His expedition had been anticipated by the rebels, particularly after he called the *ban* and *arrière-ban,* and he entered the city without resistance: Oppède's detractors had fled. In the end, a total of seventeen nobles were prosecuted and punished for their roles in the uprising. As Kettering concludes, "There was a high percentage of nobles in Aix, and their presence in the Parlement and municipal government contributed to the unruliness of these bodies."[30]

The nobility of Aix, formidably situated in provincial institutions, thus led insurrections in 1630, 1649, and 1659, all of which they justi-

28. Kettering, *Judicial Politics,* 74–76, 306, 313.

29. Kettering, *Patrons, Brokers, and Clients,* 60–61; Kettering, *Judicial Politics,* 313–14.

30. Kettering, *Judicial Politics,* 315–26.

fied as opposition to the centralization of royal authority and infringements on traditional regional privileges. In reality, they were
violently pursuing their own narrow political interests. Assisted by
the structure of provincial government and its concentration in Aix,
they dominated regional politics and these three insurrections to
their own ends. In all three incidents their efforts were colored by
factionalism that limited their effectiveness and ultimately contributed to their defeat. As elsewhere in France, the second half of the
seventeenth century saw royal agents obtain control of provincial
government—the growth of effective, absolute monarchy is, after
all, the story of Louis XIV's reign. But until 1659 the resistance
offered by noble factions in Aix and their role in provincial government essentially checked monarchial power in Provence. By these
obstructive efforts the Aixois typified the response of a provincial
nobility to encroachments by the ancien régime.

This is not to suggest that in Provence the interests of the crown
and the nobility never coincided. After 1659 the political scene in Aix
was dramatically different. Instead of chronic recalcitrance, one finds
a rather remarkable degree of compatibility between the interests of
the crown and those of the nobility. The king's ministers slowly constructed this rapprochement, using the elements of the patron–client
system. In her study of that system, Kettering has amply demonstrated the frequency of coincidence of interests during the seventeenth century. She describes the royal government's increasing re-
liance on newly formed administrative clienteles rather than the
clients of great nobles, and she explains how this shift in patronage
promoted the effectiveness and extended the control of the crown.
Richelieu, Mazarin, and the minister of finance, Colbert, each established ministerial clienteles and used provincial brokers to increase
political integration and thereby strengthen the central government.
In the formation of such clienteles, the ministers relied on local notables who acted as brokers, dispensing royal patronage to large
numbers of their own clients. Often, the brokers employed their personal resources on behalf of the crown as well. These men and their
clients ultimately proved more useful and more loyal than the clienteles of great nobles in accommodating the implementation of royal
policy. Strategically placed in provincial and municipal governments,
they were at once incorporated into the system of royal control and
left to dominate the politics of their region—this in lieu of the tradi-

tional patronage of great nobles and their clients, whose loyalty and service were at best uncertain and often nonexistent. By directing its patronage away from *les grands* and toward provincial notables and their clients, the state came to wield more control than ever and yet at the same time to enjoy a greater base of noble support.[31]

In Provence, Henri de Forbin-Maynier d'Oppède served both Mazarin and Colbert as a ministerial client and a provincial broker of patronage to a clientele that included several very prominent families. His services were first enlisted by Mazarin during the Fronde, and he continued to pursue the cardinal's policies until Mazarin's death in 1661. Apparently, there was much speculation that Mazarin's passing would mean the political demise of Oppède and his clientele, but such was not the case. Demonstrating his political acumen, Oppède scrambled to prove his usefulness to Colbert, in whose service he remained until Oppède himself died, in 1671. Among the Aixois who entered Oppède's clientele—and therefore benefited from his distribution of favors—were the houses of Forbin, Séguiran, Laurens, Puget, and Maynier. Rather significantly, Pierre de Coriolis-Villeneuve was also affiliated with Oppède's clientele through marriage, which indeed indicates important changes since the first half of the century: in 1629 and 1630 Pierre's grandfather had used his own clients to obstruct royal policy, and now Pierre belonged to a network of nobles who profited from ministerial patronage. This loose alliance of self-interested parties permitted Coriolis and his fellows to continue to dominate provincial politics, and yet it also assisted Mazarin and Colbert in their administrative reforms—indeed, it assisted Mazarin in reestablishing order during the Fronde. By Oppède's decision to switch sides in the civil war, Mazarin enlisted the support and services of some of the most important nobles in the province. Mazarin rewarded Oppède for his allegiance by naming him first president of the Parlement and acting intendant, an appointment that truly symbolized the changing relationship of provincial nobles and the state.[32]

Oppède's affiliation with Mazarin extended the monarchy's control specifically because Oppède's men were well placed in provincial

31. Kettering, *Patrons, Brokers, and Clients,* 233–37.
32. *Ibid.,* 62, 85–86, 40–42.

government. Through his own influence, fifteen of Oppède's relatives and clients served as consuls and assessors of Aix, which meant that they also acted as procureurs du pays. A cousin served as syndic of the nobility from 1661 to 1667. In 1666 a client was chosen as one of two noble procureurs to the Assembly of Communities, and both of the procureurs from the clergy were also Oppède's men. (The positions within the assembly were particularly useful in that they allowed Oppède to control debates.) And this was only part of his clientele; he had many other supporters, in the assembly and elsewhere—for example, in Parlement and in the Cour des Comptes, the latter including the first president, Reynaud de Séguiran. Furthermore, Oppède's influence extended to the municipal governments of Marseille, Toulon, Draguignan, and Carpentras. In addition, he profited from ties to Governor Mercoeur, who had originally recruited him, and to the provincial lieutenant general, Jean de Pontevès.[33]

Pontevès was the count de Carces, and his was an old and distinguished Provençal family. During the rebellion of 1649, Pontevès recruited three hundred of his own clients to fight with the parlementaires. Relations with individuals like Pontevès allowed Oppède's influence and power to fan throughout the province. The social origins of the nobles who fell in line behind him were mixed. Himself a president and later a first president in the Parlement, Oppède drew many of his supporters from the ranks of recently ennobled officeholding families; however, as a major power broker, he was also able to attract the older families of Aix and Provence at large, including the houses of Forbin, Laurens, Puget, Castellanes, and Pontevès. Kettering regards the Oppède machine as "an example of a geographic administrative clientele: province wide, cross-institutional, mixed noble in composition, attracted by the political power of its patron, and used as a political machine in helping him govern."[34]

Provincial ruling elites collaborated with the regime of Louis XIV in other provinces as well. William Beik's study of state and aristocracy in Languedoc during the seventeenth century is a highly revealing one. In Beik's opinion, the success of Louis XIV and his minis-

---

33. *Ibid.*, 100–101, 86–87.

34. *Ibid.*, 36, 87. Kettering provides a diagram of the major components in Oppède's clientele, *ibid.*, table 2, p. 88.

ters derived from their defense of traditional ruling-class interests. Provincial nobles cooperated with the crown because it was to their advantage to do so—that is, because the crown bestowed on them the offices and positions that were crucial to the implementation of royal policies, and rewarded them for jobs well done. By reinforcing class rule and hierarchy in a variety of ways, Louis XIV established order in Languedoc and integrated its ruling class into the absolutist state. Beik writes that during the reign of Louis XIV, "it was perfectly clear that hierarchy would be reinforced, the claim of the privileged to their share of society's resources would be guaranteed, and collaboration would be properly rewarded."[35]

Oppède and company were quicker than most to recognize and profit from these political realities, and Beik's description of absolutisum in Languedoc applies to Provence as well. Rather than dramatically overhaul a system of government in which political power was a function of social privilege, Louis XIV and his ministers simply assumed control of that system, thus enabling themselves to exercise initiative from within it. But in order to gain and maintain this control, they necessarily had to recognize and protect the interests of the nobility. Along the way the king's agents were able to make some reforms, such as those that promoted efficiency in tax collection, but the system remained fundamentally the same. Louis XIV's major administrative achievement was his harnessing of an existing political power structure.

A similar interweaving of interests applied in the realm of defense. Service in the "reserved occupation" of arms traditionally reinforced the privileged status of noble families while simultaneously serving the monarchy's need for security—a need that was especially acute in the frontier province of Provence. Conventional historical interpretations assert that military necessity gave rise to the French aristocracy, a privileged warrior class whose purpose was the defense of society. As Montaigne wrote, "The proper and only essential place for the nobility of France is the military profession." It is not surprising that historians who have written about the decline of the French aristocracy in the sixteenth century have posited a close

---

35. William Beik, *Absolutism and Society in Seventeenth-Century France: State Power and Provincial Aristocracy in Languedoc* (Cambridge, Eng., 1985), 31–33, 333–36.

relationship between changes in early modern armies and the alleged crisis of the nobility. They attribute to the revolution in modern warfare—the invention of gunpowder, the rise of the common infantryman—the end of a military rationale for the noble class. As evidence of the aristocracy's waning military importance, these historians cite the infrequent use of the *ban* and *arrière-ban* after the middle of the sixteenth century. Moreover, they assert that the presence of anoblis in the officer corps bastardized what was formerly an elite aristocratic cadre. One of the underlying assumptions, of course, is that old and new families never assimilated.[36]

An alternative view is possible: that even though the nature of warfare changed in the early modern period, nobles adapted easily and continued to send their sons into military careers. Members of more than half the noble families in Aix served in the royal army and navy during the seventeenth century; forty-six families had sons (often more than one) in the army or navy.[37] Of these families, twenty-six were old nobility and twenty were new. Military service was clearly not a monopoly of the old families'; instead, like the courts, it was simply another area in which old and new families of similar wealth participated more or less equally. By holding commissions in the rapidly growing army and navy of an emerging absolutist state, families such as the Coriolis and the Séguirans continued to fulfill the traditional military role of the nobility.

As the *grand maître et surintendant* of the navy and as the architect of an ambitious foreign policy, Richelieu was dedicated to creating a formidable French sea power. Because of its coastal location, Provence figured prominently in the cardinal's plans, and its nobles distinguished themselves by service to the fleet. Several of the Séguirans enjoyed illustrious careers in His Majesty's navy, and Henri de Séguiran was particularly accomplished, having commanded vessels at La Rochelle in 1622 and in the Levant in 1632. His successes in both campaigns influenced Richelieu's decision in 1633 to select Lieu-

36. Davis Bitton offers a summary of these ideas in *French Nobility in Crisis,* 27–41. As regards the "privileged warrior class," I discuss in Chapter I the fact that the southern aristocracy evolved in an entirely different manner from the nobility of northern France, giving rise to many differences that persisted through the seventeenth century.

37. Artefeuil, *Histoire héroïque et universelle,* I, II, *passim;* BDR, IV, Pt. 2.

tenant General de Séguiran for the task of inspecting the ports and coastal fortifications of Provence and monitoring traffic to and from the Levant. No doubt Séguiran's capability also persuaded Richelieu to engage his services as a client. Regrettably, Séguiran found France's southeastern fortifications to be seriously deficient; he reported to Richelieu that the situation at the port of Toulon was critical, adding that the commanding officer had nothing for a garrison but his wife and his servant.[38]

Henri de Séguiran's brother Gaspard commanded the galley *La Séguirane,* christened in the family's honor. In 1637 Gaspard was killed in combat, and the ship's command passed to Henri's son, Reynaud. With time Reynaud was promoted to lieutenant general by the duke of Mercoeur, and in 1657 he assumed the office of grand master of navigation. Anthoine de Séguiran, Reynaud's brother, served in the royal army as a captain of the guards and later as a brigadier general. Following their outstanding military careers, Henri, Reynaud, and Anthoine each in turn occupied the office of first president in the Cour des Comptes.[39] That they moved easily from military to office-holding duties, distinguishing themselves in both, discredits the idea of an occupational fissure. The Séguirans, like many Aixois, could use the sword or wear the robe, as circumstance required.

The Coriolis also shifted routinely between the army and the courts. Honoré de Coriolis, who recovered his father's office of president in Parlement following the Cascaveoux affair, held a commission in the royal army before moving to the court. His family's military tradition extended as far back as its progenitor in Aix, Jean de Coriolis, who served on a galley of Malta around 1450. As noted in Chapter II, Honoré's grandfather, a president in Parlement, lost a leg in combat, and the military services of Honoré's son, Pierre de Coriolis-Villeneuve, were rewarded when the family's fief of Espinouse was raised to a marquisat. Pierre later became a president in Parlement, and like many noble sons, he waited to assume his father's position in the court by serving first in the army.[40]

Three of Pierre's brothers, Laurent, François, and Louis, also carried on the family's military tradition by entering the chivalric order

38. Bourde, "La Provence baroque," 274; BDR, IV, Pt. 2, pp. 450–51.
39. BDR, IV, Pt. 2, pp. 450–51.
40. *Ibid.,* 147–48; Allemand, *La haute société aixoise,* 57.

Saint-Jean de Malte in 1653.[41] Established in the late eleventh century, Saint-Jean de Malte was originally an order of hospitalers. Provence had the order's oldest and largest chapter, enlisting over the centuries the sons of many noble families. Customarily, a young man entered at the age of seventeen. He took vows of poverty, chastity, and obedience—although if he chose later to marry or to change professions, he could still retain the title of chevalier. Obviously, families gained important social advantages by association with the order; indeed, by the seventeenth century, tradition and status were the real reasons for its continued popularity. Families could also use the order to groom their younger sons for coveted benefices in the Church.[42]

To be eligible for the order of Saint-Jean de Malte, a family had to provide conclusive evidence of long-standing nobility, that is, they had to demonstrate "eight quarters." In Provence this meant that the family had to prove 116 years of nobility in both the paternal and maternal lines, or nobility dating to the great-great-grandfather. Undoubtedly, there were families whose sons entered the order fraudulently, but the stringent rules for eligibility still prevented many new families from gaining admission in the seventeenth century. The names of thirty-nine noble families appear on the roles of Saint-Jean de Malte for this period; they include twenty-seven old families and twelve new families.[43] The total numbers of members drawn from old and new families, however, reveal a much more dramatic discrepancy. New families sent only 49 young men into the order during the century, whereas old families placed 260 sons there (see table 13). Included in the roll were six Coriolis, seven Guirans, and five Séguirans. The Mazargues were excluded by virtue of their Jewish ancestry, and the Beaumonts were much too recently ennobled to have been admitted during this period (interestingly, a François de Beaumont does appear on the roll for the sixteenth century, but his parentage is unknown). The decade-by-decade enrollment of both old and new families in the seventeenth century reveals a distinct difference between them, if not an area of stratification within this urban elite.

It appears that Saint-Jean de Malte excluded many anoblis simply

41. IAD, Bouches-du-Rhône, Sér. H, *Catalogue des chevaliers de Saint-Jean*, ed. M. Le Comte de Grasset (Paris, 1869), 68.

42. *Ibid.*, 10–11; Allemand, *La haute société aixoise*, 88–89.

43. Allemand, *La haute société aixoise*, 77–79; Cubells, *La Provence des Lumières*, 87; IAD, Bouches-du-Rhône, Sér. H, *Catalogue des chevaliers de Saint-Jean, passim.*

TABLE 13

Entrance in Order of Chevaliers de Malte

Decade	Sons of Old Families	Sons of New Families
1600	14	0
1610	21	2
1620	26	5
1630	46	2
1640	20	5
1650	29	5
1660	34	7
1670	22	7
1680	23	3
1690	25	11
Total	260	47
Sixteenth-Century Total	184	2

Source: IAD, Sér. H, *Catalogue des chevaliers de Saint-Jean,* ed. M. Le Compte de Grasset (Paris, 1869), *passim.*

by its emphasis on antiquity of family. In the seventeenth century, particularly the first half of the period, most anoblis lacked the long heritage of nobility required for membership. This is confirmed particularly by the fact that the young men from the twelve new families who succeeded in joining the order did so primarily during the latter part of the century. In short, this chivalric order appears to have presented one of the few barriers to upward social mobility in Aix, and this because of its emphasis on antiquity.

As a traditional symbol of noble status, membership in Saint-Jean de Malte served a dual purpose: it established within elite society the fact of a specified degree of antiquity, and it established within society as a whole the fact of elite and therefore privileged status. As a traditional prerogative of provincial nobility, domination of provincial government and politics also came to serve two purposes: it distinguished these noble families politically from their social inferiors, and by the second half of the seventeenth century, it saw them enter the service of Louis XIV's regime. The second half of the seventeenth century was much more tranquil than the first in Aix, but not because the town's most unruly residents were so stunned or intimidated by the king and his intendants that they were rendered politically harmless. It is undeniable that Louis knew the value and use of intimidation, but it is also clear that he fully understood the political virtues of an elaborate system of rewards. It was reward rather than punishment that allowed Louis to establish control over the nobility of Aix and therefore over the province. Control in "le style Louis XIV" was designed to be a mutually beneficial phenomenon.

VII

EDUCATION AND LETTERS

Perhaps no more threatening obstacle confronted the old nobility in the sixteenth century than their traditional antipathy to letters. Indeed, the crisis historians hold that educational discrepancies contributed to the cleavage between sword and robe, and that the old nobility lost ground because their anti-intellectualism and their long-standing devotion to arms left them unequipped for the venal offices of the sixteenth century, an unfortunate flaw that excluded them from early modern avenues of political power and social prestige. Davis Bitton reflects this interpretation in the statement, "Their boorishness was notorious, giving rise to the frequent charge that they had disqualified themselves by illiteracy, backwardness, and general incompetence." Bitton speculates that with proper education nobles might have been able to compete for offices with ambitious members of the middle class on the basis of merit, but he states with assurance that the requisite educational program was not followed by the old nobility. As evidence, he and others offer the works of numerous sixteenth-century writers, noble and non-noble, who criticized the old aristocracy for their pervasive ignorance.[1]

For Huppert's "gentry," conversely, education was the mainspring. It instructed them in nobility—true nobility, the idea of virtue as treated in the classics. Their ideal of nobility was therefore classical and bore little resemblance to the contemporary realities of noblesse, a distinction that they consciously cultivated. As Huppert writes, "The problem, then, was to invent an ideal of the noble life that was distinct from bourgeois life and yet not to be confused with

---

1. Bitton, *French Nobility in Crisis*, 46–48, 62–63.

the terrible image of the purely genealogical nobility—abhorred and, besides, inaccessible."[2] By education and classical ideals, the anoblis sought to separate themselves on the one hand from their mercantile origins and on the other from the warrior aristocracy, whose lack of true nobility inspired in the "gentry" nothing but contempt. In this way the educational gap between old and new contributed still further to the alleged disparity between them.

Certainly, the backwardness of the traditional nobility was the subject of many pamphlets and treatises in the sixteenth and early seventeenth centuries. Much of this literature, however, was written by noble apologists who, although pointing out the shortcomings of the French aristocracy, wrote also to propose a program for their rehabilitation. Schalk has called attention to the extent and significance of this literature, citing in many cases the same authors as Bitton. He and Bitton both, for example, rely on the work of François de L'Alouette, a lawyer who in 1577 lamented the fact that the nobility had lost virtue and was therefore losing offices and public positions to those who were better educated.[3] The difference between Bitton and Schalk in this case is one of emphasis, Bitton stressing the criticism implicit in L'Alouette's remarks, Schalk the advice.

In a similar vein, the much-better-known François de La Noue called for an academy to educate and thereby reform the nobility. La Noue surmised that because of the decadence of the class, important offices eluded the nobles and passed into the hands of those who had the necessary money and education. Rather than mere critics, La Noue and many other writers like him had an agenda for the restoration of lost virtue, one that involved, among other things, education of the nobility. Schalk considers this literature part of a *prise de conscience* that took place among the nobility in the late sixteenth century, with implications that went profoundly beyond the old aristocracy's attempts to stop the erosion of its political power.[4] He believes that the very meaning of nobility was shifting from a medieval one of function to a modern one of birth and culture, and that by the second half of the seventeenth century nobility was commonly associated with letters.

2. Huppert, *Les Bourgeois Gentilshommes,* 90.
3. Schalk, *From Valor to Pedigree,* 73–74; Bitton, *French Nobility in Crisis,* 48.
4. Schalk, *From Valor to Pedigree,* 85, 175–76.

Many sixteenth-century critics of the French nobility, in sum, wrote to encourage their subjects to reform, not simply to condemn their backwardness. Some writers even argued that education should be a preserve of the nobility, that it was necessary preparation for the military and political duties of noblemen. By the late sixteenth century a body of literature had emerged that addressed the compatibility of arms and letters and urged nobles to tap the wealth of knowledge and experience available in literature, particularly the classics. Here appears the influence of humanism on the education of the nobility and on the culture of early modern France. The humanists designed a program to make virtuous men by classical example. Such an education would produce not only good or "noble" men, but men equipped to participate in public life. William Harrison Woodward suggests that humanism was actually grafted onto the knightly ideal to produce something new—an aristocratic ideal that combined both arms and letters.[5] Thus the definition of nobility acquired a cultural component.

The practical reason for advocating (and undergoing) reform was, of course, to maintain political power in changing political and military circumstances. One of the first historians to look at this kind of reform was J. H. Hexter, writing primarily about England and France. He argues that the growth of government and the evolution of the state necessarily changed the nobilities of England and France. For example, the education of young nobles came to be seen in a new light, as valuable training for administrative positions in the rapidly expanding bureaucracies of the sixteenth century. As early as the reign of Henry VIII, young English aristocrats matriculated in large numbers at the Inns of Court. In sixteenth-century England gentlemen believed that it was their duty to assume possession of the many offices that were emerging. Obviously, ignorance would be a fatal encumbrance in this process. Hexter in fact sees a condemnation of indifference to letters as a signal sixteenth-century contribution to the evolution and survival of the aristocracies of the two kingdoms. He poses a very important question: "How prostrate is a social group

5. John David Nordhaus, *Arma et Litterae: The Education of the Noblesse de Race in Sixteenth-Century France,* Microfilm (Ann Arbor, 1974), 150, 152; Joan Simon, *Education and Society in Tudor England* (Cambridge, Mass., 1966), 64; William Harrison Woodward, *Studies in Education During the Age of the Renaissance, 1400–1600* (Cambridge, Eng., 1906), 246.

that, facing the challenge of new times, rises to meet it by engaging in an altogether new kind of activity—that of acquiring a kind of learning hitherto almost monopolized by clerics?"[6]

The French nobility also met the challenge of new times and the threat of new elements in society by tending to the great matter of education. Schalk emphasizes the important role that noble academies played in changing the image of aristocracy. In addition, French nobles attended the universities for the legal training necessary to assuming their proper place in public life.[7] Seventeenth-century Aix was the site of one of these noble academies, and large numbers of nobles also attended the local university. Significantly, an interest in education was not a recent development among the native noble families of Aix. For the anoblis, of course, education had been essential to their social progress. After all, they had started the process of moving upward as successful entrepreneurs or as local attorneys and notaries, all of which required more than mere functional literacy. Nor was education any novelty to the old families of Aix. As city dwellers they had long since recognized education's virtues, and in this way too they bore a closer resemblance to the patriciate of an Italian city-state than to the rural, feudal elite of northern France. The old noble families of Aix, despite their fiefholding, membership in chivalric orders, and military service, had never really conformed to the sword model; they were not really warriors and their interests were not particularly rural. Preferring to live in town and occasionally engaging in trade, they maintained cultural interests akin to those of urban elites elsewhere in the Mediterranean world. By the standards of the northern squirearchy, the Aixois exhibited a degree of education and cultivation that was almost by definition the product of city dwelling.

In early modern Europe the obvious criterion that distinguished the educated from the great unwashed was the ability to read and write, and contemporary critics of the French aristocracy were appalled by its broad lack of even basic literacy. For much of the pro-

6. J. H. Hexter, *Reappraisals in History: New Views of History and Society in Early Modern Europe* (New York, 1961), 45–70.

7. Schalk, *From Valor to Pedigree,* Chap. 8; Nordhaus, *Arma et Litterae,* 118; Dewald, *Formation of a Provincial Nobility,* 22–26; Roger Chartier, Dominique Julia, and Marie-Madeleine Compère, *L'education en France du XVIe au XVIIIe siècle* (Paris, 1976), 169.

vincial nobility of France, illiteracy was undoubtedly a function of their rural existence. During the sixteenth and seventeenth centuries, literacy rates were almost always higher in towns and cities than in the countryside. R. A. Houston attributes the difference to the fact that cities by their very nature attracted literate categories of people—merchants, professionals, certain craftsmen—and to what he calls a "hothouse" effect arising out of "the concentration of cultural features associated with reading and writing." But the more literate environment of towns did not derive solely from the concentration of literate people in a limited geographical area; a comparison of literacy rates for town dwellers and country residents in the same social groups indicates that urban life provided greater opportunities to learn to read and write even for those whose education would certainly have been neglected in rural areas.[8]

Of course, even within this context of urban opportunities, literacy conformed to social and economic structures. Obviously, wealth and privilege afforded greater access to education than did poverty and hardship. In fact, the ability to read and write reinforced social distinctions because it infiltrated society "from the top downwards." In his study of the history of literacy, Harvey Graff refers to eighteenth-century Provence as an example of this pattern. By the beginning of the century, the notables of the towns were almost all literate, while their social inferiors trailed substantially behind.[9] Aix both follows this pattern and confirms the notion of literacy as a function of urban development. As an administrative capital it offered its inhabitants far better prospects for literacy than did most places, but even there the elite, as ever, had the best prospects of all.

Chapters V and VI addressed the political implications of urban residence and the fact that city life offered elites unique opportunities

8. R. A. Houston, *Literacy in Early Modern Europe: Culture and Education, 1500–1800* (London, 1988), 137–45.

9. *Ibid.,* 150; François Furet and Jacques Ozouf, *Reading and Writing: Literacy in France from Calvin to Jules Ferry* (New York, 1982), 149–50; Harvey Graff, *The Legacies of Literacy: Continuities and Contradictions in Western Culture and Society* (Bloomington, 1987), 212–15. It should be noted that in his remarks about eighteenth-century Provence, Graff relied on the findings of Michel Vovelle, "Y a-t-il eu une révolution culturelle au XVIIIe siècle? A propos de l'education populaire en Provence," *Revue d'Histoire Moderne et Contemporaine,* XXII (1975), 100–103.

for political power. These political opportunities in turn created specific incentives for education, which in turn again reinforced the elit-
ist patterns within urban culture. An educational level that surpassed
basic literacy was essential to political power within the city—a reality long since recognized by old noble families in Aix. From the
Middle Ages through the seventeenth century, these families had
served as consuls, assessors, and councillors in municipal government. Through the fifteenth century they had participated in the
government of the counts of Provence. After 1501 and the creation of
the Parlement, they had served as magistrates in the sovereign courts
as well. In short, their history of political activity suggests a level of
education and sophistication traditionally reserved by historians for
the noblesse de robe.

In his study of the parlementaires of Rouen, Dewald writes that the
education of a magistrate was cosmopolitan. It began with a year or
two of studies at home, followed perhaps by instruction from a private schoolmaster. Then, at about age twelve, the child enrolled at a
collège, or secondary school, for several years of Latin studies. From
the collège it was on to the university to study law. There the student
became familiar with the elements of Roman law, gained an understanding of legal theory, and was imbued with an appreciation for
the historical context of the law.[10] In Aix this was an educational program for old and new families alike. Old and new families shared
offices in the courts, invested in the same forms of wealth, and intermarried routinely. And both received similar educations, enabling
them to serve equally in government.

Legal training acquired at the University of Aix prepared many
young noblemen for the Parlement and the Cours des Comptes. The
university, created in 1409, flourished during the fifteenth century
under the patronage of the counts of Provence. In the sixteenth century war and disease disrupted the town and threatened to destroy
the school; it was saved only by the intervention of the provincial
Estates, which approved a sales tax on wine to maintain the faculties
of law, theology, and medicine. In 1583 the Estates also founded a
collège in Aix for instruction in the humanities, thereby expanding

10. Dewald, *Formation of a Provincial Nobility,* 22–27.

the available educational facilities to accommodate the humanist program.[11]

Louis XIII added to educational opportunities in Aix in 1611 by establishing a noble academy. Among the officially stated reasons for its foundation was the necessity to combine arms and letters, a goal regarded as being especially desirable in this frontier province: the monarchy hoped by education to teach respect and loyalty before such virtues were instilled by foreigners (in this case the Italians and the Spanish). Nobles who attended the academy in Aix studied horsemanship and arms, but they also received instruction in mathematics, writing, dancing, and music. Thus, by the early seventeenth century, various avenues existed for the education of young noblemen in Aix. As the historian Pitton wrote in 1666, everything necessary to produce an *honnête homme* was being taught there.[12]

It is clear from the records of the university that by the seventeenth century many young nobles were taking advantage of these facilities. The register of the university indicates the number of terminal degrees granted to members of the local nobility, that is, to the eighty-one extended families.[13] During the century thirty of the thirty-eight old noble families had members who graduated from the university. In fact, these thirty families earned a total of 141 terminal degrees, 94 of which were doctorates in law or theology. The university register lists the names of thirty-seven of the forty-three new families for a total of 119 final degrees, 90 being doctorates.

Although the figures for the old nobility compare favorably with those for the anoblis, they do not present the complete picture of higher education among the Aixois because many families sent sons to universities elsewhere, or to the academy of Aix. Nevertheless, the closely parallel achievements of the two groups at the university do imply that by the seventeenth century there was no discrepancy between the educational levels of the old nobility and the new; any gap that might previously have existed had closed.

11. Hastings Rashdall, *The Universities of Europe in the Middle Ages* (2 vols.; Oxford, Eng., 1895), II, 184–87; Jean Scholastique Pitton, *Histoire de la ville d'Aix* . . . (Aix, 1660), 593–94.

12. Schalk, *From Valor to Pedigree*, 188–92; Pitton, *Histoire de la ville d'Aix*, 593–94.

13. ADBR, Aix, "Répertoire alphabétique des gradués de l'Université d'Aix, 1531–1791," I–V.

The contributions that the Aixois made to maintain the various facilities offer additional evidence of their interest in education. Huppert has written that the nobility's interest in the collèges was extremely limited and that nobles rarely acted as benefactors. Aix, however, contradicts these assertions. The collège records identify a long list of benefactors during the seventeenth century. These individuals were almost exclusively noble, and they came from old families as often as from new. They made their contributions in various forms, the most common being the simple donation of money. Some nobles also established *pensions* or bonds in the name of the collège. In 1629, for example, Lazarin du Suffren, who came from an old established family, donated 720 livres for an annual *pension* to the school, then followed this generous gift with a *don gratuit* of 300 livres. Other nobles used their testaments to bequeath portions of their estates to the collège.[14]

These various contributions reflect not only an interest in education, but the fact that education was a matter of civic concern. In Chapter V, I discussed how both old families and anoblis participated in the municipal life of Aix, serving on the town council, the Bureau of Police, the Bureau of Health, and the administrative boards of charities. Together they funded much of the municipal debt and indisputably dominated town life. For the nobility of Aix, the university was simply another aspect of urban life to be supported with charitable contributions. A sense of civic responsibility, combined with a recognition of the value of education, inspired a concern for the affairs and welfare of the local educational facilities.

If the records of the university and the collège manifest the overall importance that the resident nobility assigned to education, the inventories of individual nobles' libraries indicate some of their specific intellectual interests. These inventories are interspersed in the vast collection of notary documents in Aix. Although it would be naïve to assume that the owner actually read every book he possessed, the contents of a library do provide an idea of the interests and background of the person to whom it belonged; the very fact of ownership suggests this.

14. Huppert, *Les Bourgeois Gentilshommes*, 67; ADBR, Aix, Edouard Méchin, ed., "L'enseignement en Provence avant la Révolution. Annales du Collège Royal Bourbon d'Aix depuis les premières démarches faits pour sa fondation jusqu'au 7 Ventose an III époque de sa suppression. Manuscrits et documents originaux," I, II, *passim*.

Judging from the inventories of twelve libraries in Aix, the general content of the collections did not vary significantly with the antiquity of the family. For example, books dealing with law and jurisprudence were numerous in the libraries of both old and new families—hardly surprising in a town where most noble families had members serving in the royal courts. Legal works constituted 21 percent of the volumes in the libraries of old noble families and 28 percent of the volumes in the libraries of anoblis. Typical materials included the laws and *coutumiers* of the various regions of France, ordinances by the king, and the *arrêts* of the Parlement of Paris. A small portion of the legal literature in each library dealt with canon and ecclesiastical law, but Roman law figured much more prominently: copies of the *Codex Justinianus* were common, as were commentaries on Roman law and treatises comparing Roman and French law. In large part this interest in Roman law reflected its profound influence on the legal traditions of southern France. Humanism also reinforced the study of Roman law, and philology undoubtedly provided jurists and scholars a more complete understanding of it. In addition, nobles owned treatises and commentaries on Salic law, on the system of taxation in France, on hereditary succession, and on criminal and civil procedure. Although the most common jurists were Loyseau, Imbert, and Lovet, the works of Alciato and Baudouin were also mentioned in several inventories, and their inclusion suggests the influence of the humanists' historical approach to the study of law.[15]

The effects of the humanist interest in the past are even more apparent in the collections of history and political theory, which made up 24 percent of the contents of the libraries of the old families and 18 percent of the libraries of the anoblis. Nobles were particularly interested in the histories of Rome and France, but they read about other kingdoms and civilizations as well. Their libraries contained many studies of historical figures, especially the kings of France. Books on Charles VII, Louis IX, and Henry IV were numerous, as were studies of individuals close to the throne, such as the duke of Sully, Cardinal Richelieu, and the Medici. Among classical subjects,

15. The twelve inventories of noble libraries were found in ADBR, Aix, Fonds Lévy-Bram, 303E-562, 303E-563, 303E-564, 303E-566, 303E-568, and 303E-569. The twelve families to which these inventories belonged included five old noble families and seven new noble families.

Alexander the Great and Julius Caesar dominated, with copies of Caesar's *Commentaries* appearing in most of the libraries. The inventory of Pierre Dedons, écuyer d'Aix and a member of an old and politically important family, reveals how humanism, with its emphasis on history, influenced the intellectual interests of the older nobility. His library held histories of Rome, France, Spain, Portugal, and Flanders, in addition to works on the Turks, the popes, and Julius Caesar. He also owned books on more contemporary historical topics, such as the Wars of Religion in France, the Gallican liberties, Richelieu, and the memoirs of Sully.[16]

Accompanying the historical works were many volumes on political theory. The Aixois were, not surprisingly, interested in the issue of royal authority and sovereignty and read authors such as Claude de Seyssel and François Hotman. In addition, their libraries contained several anonymous treatises on the origins of the authority of the Estates of France. Machiavelli and Jean Bodin were the most widely read of the contemporary political theorists, but four works by Hugo Grotius, a French edition of Thomas More's *Utopia,* and a volume entitled *The Politics of Hobbes* also appear on the lists. The Aixois obviously had a strong interest in history and political theory—an interest that derived in part from the emphasis that humanists gave to these subjects—and the works they owned on those subjects were well suited to the new political realities of the age in which they lived.

Although the humanist influence clearly existed in the areas of law, history, and political theory, its most obvious manifestation was in the abundance of writings by classical authors, whose works formed the third-largest category of literature in the twelve libraries. Again, there was little difference between the libraries of old and new families; classical titles constituted 11 percent of the volumes owned by the former and 15 percent of those belonging to the latter. For the French nobility in general, an emphasis on classical texts was a critical part of the process by which the meaning of *noblesse* was changing from one of function to one based on culture, that is, the classical influence was a major component in the program for the nobility's rehabilitation. For the Aixois, however, interest in the classics was indigenous and genuine; as participants in an inherently literate cul-

16. ADBR, Aix, Fonds Lévy-Bram, 303E-562, 1655–56, pp. 560–817.

ture, they were capable of appreciating and sharing in the revival of classical antiquity, and not simply as a remedy, but for its cultural value. No library was without at least one copy of Cicero; all but one family owned editions of Plutarch, Seneca, and Ovid; and some of the families had several works of these classical authors. Young noblemen in Aix had become familiar with Plutarch, Cicero, and Virgil as they studied Latin in school. As adults they also read Tacitus, Pliny, Livy, Horace, Terence, Marcus Aurelius, Quintilian, and Suetonius. Aristotle was the most prominent Greek author in the inventories, but works by Plato were not uncommon, and two families owned copies of Homer.

Works by the proponents of classicism, the humanists themselves, were also well represented in the libraries, especially those by Erasmus and Pico della Mirandola. The inventories recorded two works of Marsilio Ficino but, rather amazingly, none of either Lefèvre d'Etaples or Rabelais; perhaps the many copies of Montaigne compensated somewhat for those absences. The inclusion of authors such as Copernicus, Ariosto, Tasso, Corneille, and Malherbe gives further testimony that the nobility's intellectual interests were current and that their literary tastes were not limited to the authors taught in school.

While the nobles of Aix read the classical and contemporary authors prescribed for the rehabilitation of the French aristocracy, they also continued to read about warfare and other topics traditionally associated with nobility. The volume of literature on warfare had actually increased significantly in the late sixteenth century, at the very time when the military rationale for a nobility was supposedly in decline. It has been suggested that the publication of numerous treatises on the art of war signaled an early response to the critics of the nobility—that is, it was the first step toward the conjoining of arms and letters.[17] In seventeenth-century Aix the libraries of nobles included works on fortification, artillery, infantry, and various other aspects of the military arts. Lasard du Chaine, for example, owned several such volumes, including a copy of Pluvinel's *Instruction . . . for Mounting a Horse*.[18] Du Chaine, like the Séguirans, is a fine example of the assimilation that had taken place in Aix. Although the du Chaines'

17. Nordhaus, *Arma et Litterae,* Chap. 4; Schalk, *From Valor to Pedigree,* Chap. 8.
18. ADBR, Fonds Lévy-Bram, 303E-566, 1662–63, 1138–1276.

claims to nobility had not been firmly established until the sixteenth century, the family had become quite prominent and engaged in activities usually associated with the old, traditional nobility. As both president in Parlement and a chevalier de Malte, Lasard epitomized the blend of interests that was so common among nobles in seventeenth-century Aix. Besides his books on warfare, he also owned the single most impressive collection of legal works.

In addition to reading about warfare, du Chaine and the other nobles studied chivalry, honor, and courtesy—topics associated with the old aristocracy. Books of this nature, together with those on warfare, constituted 4 percent of the books in the libraries of both old and new noble families. Although the twelve inventories recorded only one copy of Castiglione, there were several anonymous manuals of courtesy modeled after his epochally influential *The Courtier* and entitled simply *L'honnête homme*. The same sort of courtesy manuals existed for sons, daughters, wives, and widows, and some of them were quite specific in the topics they addressed—one, for example, was entitled *The Duties of the Son at the Funeral of His Father*.

From the lofty fields of chivalry, honor, and courtesy, nobles sometimes departed for lighter reading that might be construed as seventeenth-century pornography. The same Lasard du Chaine owned a rather substantial collection of books whose titles are fairly suggestive. They include *The Manual of Love, Amorous Passions,* and *The Delectable Folly*. He also seems to have been interested in the battle between the sexes, as he owned copies of *The War Between Men and Women* and *The Defence of Women Against the Alphabet of Their Imperfections*. One last title, *On the Dissolution of Marriage by Impotence,* suggests that du Chaine might have been a casualty of that battle.[19]

In an appropriate counterpoint to such patently worldly fare, the inventories also record a substantial body of religious literature, constituting 18 and 12 percent, respectively, of the libraries of old and new houses. The works ranged from inspirational literature (lives of saints and devotionals, including the *Imitation of Christ* by Thomas à Kempis) to the weighty theological works of Saint Augustine, Thomas Aquinas, and Nicolas of Cusa. Of course, there were several copies of the Bible and numerous editions of the New Testament in

19. *Ibid.*

both Greek and Latin. With the exception of a work by Cornelius Jansen, the twelve libraries contained nothing that would question the doctrinal orthodoxy of their owners.

From legal studies to the classics to the lives of saints, the contents of these twelve libraries are strikingly predictable; the inventories include precisely the authors and titles that one would expect to find in the library of an educated person of the seventeenth century. This may be the libraries' most important feature, that they reflect the intellectual atmosphere of the period, particularly the impact of humanism; for that atmosphere presupposed a well-established tradition of literacy and education. To read Cicero, Tacitus, Augustine, Ficino, and Erasmus required a level of literacy and an intellectual maturity that would certainly have been missing in only recently educated and rehabilitated minds.

Another key point is that the inventories reveal no significant difference between the collections owned by old noble families and those of anoblis. This point is particularly important in the case of books on law. Eager to assume positions in the royal courts, old noble families sent their sons to the local university for legal studies. The education that the young men received there helped them to continue in the role of a political elite by enabling them to function in the context of the early modern bureaucratic state. The legal literature that accumulated in their libraries was physical evidence of their ability to adapt to changing circumstances.

CONCLUSION

In a broad sense this work addresses three related historical questions. It asks if the French nobility had declined by the seventeenth century as a social, economic, and political force; if a functional division existed between sword and robe; and if important regional variations among provincial nobilities should be taken into consideration when addressing either of these issues. The circumstances of the nobility of Aix refute the idea of an aristocratic crisis, certainly for Aix and certainly before the reign of Louis XIV. Even after the Fronde, the Aixois nobles retained their privileged place in urban society. Nor did the end of the judicial revolts in 1659 signal the political decline of this traditional opponent of the crown. Instead, the relative tranquillity that Aix experienced in the second half of the century was in large measure the result of cooperation between the crown and the nobility, particularly those noble families who saw in this arrangement the occasion for aggrandizement by serving those close to the king as brokers of their patronage.

Kettering has shown how Richelieu, Mazarin, and Colbert recruited reliable local notables as clients and placed them within provincial administration. This was done necessarily at the exclusion of *les grands,* who later in the century would take up circumspect residence at Versailles. Acting as political brokers, the new clients distributed royal patronage to their own supporters, many of whom were Aixois; in doing so, they enabled the central government to extend political integration to provincial elites, to mobilize provincial resources, and thereby to strengthen the state. Kettering maintains that the early modern state "rested on a broader base of noble support than has generally been recognized."[1] The king and his agents had devised a system of administrative clienteles that permitted loyalty to both patron and crown, and that served mutually the needs of the state and its most privileged subjects.

As for the chasm between "sword" and "robe," the nobility of Aix, like the nobilities of Bayeux and Rouen, might be better described in other terminology. Dewald has suggested that it would be better to think of sword and robe as components of a reasonably cohesive group, rather than view France as being "dominated by a pair of fundamentally hostile elites."[2] In her study of the parlementaires of eighteenth-century Aix, Monique Cubells also emphasizes the less fractious character of this urban nobility, although she does so strictly within the context of separate sword and robe components. She writes that the comportment of the sword and the robe nobles implied equality and parallelism, not hierarchy—that there was more unity than conflict between the two. Both groups faced a common enemy: money; that is, money of a very modern, capitalistic, and highly speculative nature. This threat had a cohesive effect on their society. The sword was not eclipsed by the robe, and the robe did not suffer an inferiority complex. Warfare and justice were, after all, both traditional duties of noblemen. For Cubells, the two groups' behavior and attitudes promoted a unity of ideology or *mentalité*—in short, a true social unity.[3] But in all of this Cubells continues to use the traditional nomenclature. She still sees two components in the nobility.

I think it is possible to go a step further in the case of Aix (and much of southern France). I suggest that sword and robe were never really identifiable components there, and that old and new noble families formed a structural as well as an ideological unity. I argue that a robe nobility did not exist in Aix for the simple reason that a clearly definable sword nobility never actually existed. The old Aixois nobility, with its municipal and civic orientation, moved easily and automatically into what might have been the realm of a robe nobility. The easy association and thorough integration of families of ancient and recent lineage were essential traits of this urban nobility,

1. Kettering, *Patrons, Brokers, and Clients*, 233–34, 236.
2. Dewald, *Formation of a Provincial Nobility*, 309.
3. Cubells, *La Provence des Luminères*, chap. 7.

traits clearly promoted by the fact that both kinds of families came from the same milieu. This is not to imply that harmony reigned over their social and political lives—Kettering has documented conclusively a factionalism that promoted internal discord and general unruliness among nobles—but simply to state that antiquity of family was not an important source of hostility.

Perhaps the Aixois were unique in this regard. Certainly, their concentration in an urban environment was not typical, and it clearly nurtured similar interests between old and new families. The urban milieu offered both groups the same sources of income and investment, particularly offices in the royal bureaucracy, and this bond of common interests contributed enormously to the structural unity of this elite. It is also possible that in this case, familiarity did not breed contempt but instead encouraged integrative phenomena such as intermarriage. Although families' attitudes toward marriage were largely calculating, matches being contrived in the interest of the house, old and new families intermarried with such frequency that distinctions in antiquity became problematic.

It is reasonable to believe that the Aixois, rather than being a mere aberration, speak for much of the southern nobility, whose collective past has for so long been overlooked by historians positing models of aristocratic behavior and aristocratic ruin. Southern nobles invested and managed their wealth according to the rules of southern traditions and southern laws. In some ways this gave them an economic advantage over their northern counterparts. Cubells has suggested that the Provençaux saw in modern forms of money a threat to nobility, both sword and robe. Here, too, I disagree, at least for the seventeeth century. The Aixois exhibited considerable familiarity with modern forms of investment. They traded in bonds or rentes with such frequency and flexibility that one can only conclude a considerable degree of comfort and success with these new capitalist instruments. Particularly striking was the level of investment on the part of old families, who also held considerable wealth in fief. Their easy acceptance of less tangible forms of wealth was, I would argue, the result of their urban backgrounds. Moneylending and commerce were traditional features of the urban economy in which these families had functioned for generations. It was not a question of adapting to a new economy; for the Aixois such an economy was a sine qua non.

Moreover, the widespread existence of allodial property in Provence offered aristocratic society an alternative source of landed wealth that could be exploited in more capitalistic ways than could holdings in fief. The allod had survived in great abundance in the south because of the legal traditions of the region, specifically the impact of Roman law. These traditions not only made easier the immediate exploitation of the countryside, but at the same time provided nobles the means to preserve their gains over generations. The customs of the Midi influenced aristocratic inheritance practices in three ways: by guaranteeing for each child a share of the estate; by giving the father the power to decide in his testament how he would pay the shares, or légitimes, of his children; and by permitting the father to exclude legally any previously endowed child from part of the inheritance. Through cogent management and coordination of their testaments and marriage contracts, houses channeled vast fortunes to their principal heirs, negotiated a few strategic marriages, and yet still provided for all other family members. Testamentary management of wealth was a matter that the Aixois tended to with great seriousness and practicality, for it was as critical to the economic base of a house as was sound investment during the patriarch's lifetime.

The eighty-one native-noble families also wielded political power and social privilege in distinctly southern and municipal ways. They assumed a character more like that of an Italian patriciate than that of a French squirearchy. Through their participation in municipal government, they continued to observe the Roman custom of service to the state, while by their domination of charity and various municipal agencies, they exhibited a modern sense of noblesse oblige. The town was their milieu and they its leading citizens. Naturally, they assumed a dominant role, even at times exploiting the urban populace to further their own political ends. Privilege means control, and for the Aixois it meant specifically urban control. The cumulative effect of their civic activities was great, exerting an overwhelming influence on the urban environment.

In the final analysis it was the ability to adapt to changing circumstances that underscored the assimilation of old and new families in Aix and that permitted the resulting elite to maintain both local and regional power. Education was an integral part of the nobility's evolution, and by the seventeenth century the Aixois were a cultured group with no educational distinctions between old and new. This, too, was in part a function of their urban environment. Privilege in an urban context inherently entailed access to education, a fact that largely distinguished urban from rural society. Those who took advantage of the educational opportunities in Aix were not confined to the anoblis. The clearly defined cultural separation perceived by Huppert simply did not exist there. The anoblis were not a world apart from the old nobility, nor did they strive to achieve cultural distance from it.

Historians of France have long acknowledged the profound regional diversity and provincialism of the early modern period. In reconsidering some of the established interpretations about French society and proposing new models of societal change, today's historians must take the opportunity to accommodate these local variations. France was the sum of its parts during the ancien régime, a fact that regularly confounded the centralizing desires of the crown and those placed near it—and a fact that modern students of the time must not overlook.

APPENDIX I

Noble Families Relative to the Total Population of Aix in 1695

Group	Households	Total Inhabitants	Percentage of Population
"Seigneurs de"	50	384	1.40
Cadets, chevaliers	7	30	.11
Ecuyers	136	534	1.94
"Nobles"	88	311	1.13
Chevaliers de Malte	34	169	.61
Officiers de guerre	85	419	1.52
Prés. de Parle.	14	224	.81
Conseillers de Parle.	91	747	2.72
Avocats/procureurs gén., Parle.	6	39	.14
Prés. des Comptes	8	83	.30
Conseillers des Comptes	41	332	1.21
Avocats/procureurs gén., Comptes	5	43	.16
Auditeurs/correcteurs, Comptes	5	30	.11
Sec. du roi, Chancellerie	6	37	.13
Trésoriers gén. de France	7	53	.19
Gr. sén./lieut. sénéchal	5	38	.14
Conseillers sénéchal	4	18	.07
Avocats/procureur du roi sénéchal	1	6	.02
Viguier de la ville	2	9	.03
Consuls municipal	1	5	.02
Totals	596	3,511	12.76

Source: Based on Coste, *La Ville d'Aix en 1695*, 756–57.

APPENDIX II

Social Profiles of the Noble Families of Seventeenth-Century Aix

	Old Families			
Name	Owned Fiefs	Offices in Courts	Town Council	Married Outside Group
Arbaud	X	X	X	X
Arlatan	X	X		
Arnaud	X	X	X	X
Benaud	X	X	X	
Bompar	X	X	X	
Chailan	X	X	X	X
Clapiers	X	X	X	X
Coriolis	X	X	X	X
Cormis	X	X	X	
Dedons	X	X	X	X
Durand	X	X	X	X
Duranty	X	X	X	X
Estienne	X	X	X	X
Farges	X	X	X	X
Félix	X	X		X
Flotte	X	X	X	X
Forbin	X	X	X	X
Gaillard	X	X	X	X
Gantes	X	X	X	X
Gaufridy	X	X	X	X
Guiran	X	X	X	X
Isoard	X			
Joannis	X	X		X
Laidet	X	X	X	
Laurens	X	X	X	X
Malespine	X		X	
Martins	X		X	X
Michaelis	X	X	X	X
Ollivary	X	X	X	X
Périer	X	X	X	X
Puget	X		X	X
Quiqueron	X			
Simiane	X	X		X
Suffren	X	X		
Thomas	X	X	X	X
Thomassin	X	X	X	X
Tressemanes	X	X	X	X
Villeneuve	X	X	X	X

	New Families		
Name	Owned Fiefs	Offices in Courts	Town Council	Married Outside Group
Adaoust		X		
Agut	X	X	X	X
Albert	X	X	X	X
Antelemy		X	X	
Antoine		X	X	
Aimar	X	X	X	X
Ballon	X	X	X	X
Beaumont	X	X	X	X
Bourdon	X			
Briançon	X			X
Chaine	X	X	X	X
Croze	X	X	X	X
Desideri		X	X	X
Espagnet		X	X	X
Galice	X	X	X	X
Garnier	X	X	X	X
Gassendi	X	X	X	X
Gautier	X	X	X	X
Gilbert		X	X	
Gras	X	X		X
Guerin	X	X	X	X
Guidy		X	X	X
Honorat	X	X	X	
Maliverny	X	X	X	X
Margelet	X	X		X
Maynier	X	X	X	X
Mazargues	X	X	X	X
Menc	X	X	X	X
Meyronnet	X	X	X	
Monier	X	X	X	X
Pelicot	X		X	
Pitton	X			
Rabasse	X	X	X	X
Regis	X	X	X	X
Saint-Marc		X	X	X
Séguiran	X	X	X	X
Seillans	X			
Templeri		X	X	

	New Families			
Name	Owned Fiefs	Offices in Courts	Town Council	Married Outside Group
Thoron	X	X	X	
Tibaud	X	X		
Veteris	X		X	
Vitalis	X	X	X	
Voland	X			X

APPENDIX III

Membership of the Five Selected Families on the Town Council

Year	Guirans	Coriolis	Séguirans	Beaumonts	Marzargues
1600				1	
1601				1	
1602				1	
1603			2	3	
1604			2	2	2
1605			2	2	1
1606		1			
1607	1	1	2		
1608	1		1		
1609		1		4	
1610			2		
1611				1	
1612				1	
1613			2	3	
1614			2		
1615			1		
1616			2	2	
1617				1	
1618		1	1	2	1
1619			1	2	
1620				1	1
1621			3	2	1
1622				2	1
1623				1	
1624				1	
1625				1	
1626				1	
1627			1	1	
1628			1	1	
1629					1
1630		1		2	
1631		1		1	
1632				1	
1633				1	
1634			2		
1635				2	
1636			1	1	
1637			1	1	
1638			1	1	
1639			1	1	1

Year	Guirans	Coriolis	Séguirans	Beaumonts	Marzargues
1640			1		
1641				2	
1642		1	1	4	
1643		1		6	
1644				2	
1645				2	1
1646				1	
1647				3	
1648			1		
1649	1		2	2	
1650	1		1	2	
1651				1	
1652				3	
1653				1	
1654				2	
1655				1	
1656			1	2	
1657			1	3	
1658			1	3	
1659			1	3	
1660	1			1	
1661			1	1	
1662				2	
1663	1		1	3	
1664			1	2	
1665			1		
1666	1			3	
1667				2	
1668				1	
1669			1		
1670					
1671			2	1	
1672			2	1	
1673			1		
1674			1	2	
1675			1		
1676			1	1	
1677			1		1
1678	1			1	1
1679				2	

Year	Guirans	Coriolis	Séguirans	Beaumonts	Marzargues
1680				2	
1681					
1682				1	
1683				1	
1684					1
1685					1
1686					1
1687					
1688					1
1689					
1690					1
1691					1
1692					1
1693					
1694	1			1	
1695	1				

Source: AC, Aix, BB99–BB105, Délibérations du Conseil.

APPENDIX IV

Revenues from Fiefholding, 1668

Old Families	Total revenue	New Families	Total revenue
Arbaud*	NA	Adaoust	0**
Arlatan*	NA	Agut	4,050
Arnaud	4,200	Albert	530
Benaud*	NA	Antelemy	0
Bompar*	NA	Antoine	0
Chailan	600	Aimar	2,900
Clapiers	8,400	Ballon*	NA
Coriolis	7,840	Beaumont	100
Cormis	1,630	Bourdon	500
Dedons	1,800	Briançon*	NA
Durand	850	Chaine	4,300
Duranty	400	Croze	2,500
Estienne	2,000	Desideri	0
Farges*	NA	Espagnet	0
Félix	5,027	Galice	275
Flotte	1,450	Garnier	2,650
Forbin	28,100	Gassendi	942
Gaillard	6,754	Gautier	2,025
Gantes*	NA	Gilbert	0
Gaufridy	1,800	Gras	300
Guiran	3,050	Guerin	700
Isoard	5,150	Guidy	0
Joannis	10	Honorat	100
Laidet	4,300	Maliverny*	NA
Laurens	5,250	Margelet*	NA
Malespine*	NA	Maynier	360
Martins	2,000	Mazargues*	NA
Michaelis*	NA	Menc	900
Ollivary*	NA	Meyronnet*	NA
Périer	805	Monier	153
Puget	10,394	Pelicot*	NA
Quiqueron*	NA	Pitton	775
Simiane	300	Rabasse	900
Suffren*	NA	Regis	250
Thomas	2,820	Saint-Marc	0
Thomassin	4,300	Séguiran	300
Tressemanes	1,443	Seillans	2,400
Villeneuve	18,025	Templeri	0
Total	128,698	Thoron	2,400
		Tibaud	NA
		Veteris	NA

146

Old Families	Total revenue	New Families	Total revenue
		Vitalis	850
		Voland	848
		Total	32,008

*Families that held fiefs and were not listed in the 1668 afflorinement. Information on the number of their fiefs was compiled from the following sources: B. Méjanes, MS 1133 (R.A. 32) "Jugement de la noblesse de Provence"; MS 733-737 (829-833-R.449, 723, 724) Recueil de pièces sur la Provence, II; "Etat et rolle des lettres patentes acquités . . . aux acquéreurs des fiefs de 1626 à 1680"; Artefeuil, *Histoire héroïque et universelle.*
**0 (zero) indicates no holdings in fief.
Source: B. Méjanes, MS 1143 (630-R.732), "Etat du florinage . . . 1668." The figures on revenue in Appendix IV are based solely on this source.

BIBLIOGRAPHY

The research for this study was done largely in Aix at the annex of the Archives Départementales des Bouches-du-Rhône. Housed in this archive is a voluminous collection of notarial records for the seventeenth century, the largest single source consulted in the course of my research and one whose extent prohibits listing each volume separately. For a given notary of the period, a volume of several hundred pages usually exists for each year in his career; multiplied by twenty or thirty years, his work may constitute a small collection in itself. Fortunately for me and others working with notarial records, archivists have laboriously cataloged each notary's work as part of a larger collection or *fond*, making it easier to cite such documents. I have therefore listed concisely all notary material by collections or *fonds* rather than by notary or volume. Sources that I consulted at the Bibliothèque Méjanes in Aix are listed by manuscript number and title. I also cited in the same manner the long series of annual records for town government and municipal agencies located in the Archives Communales of Aix.

PRIMARY SOURCES
Archival Sources

Archives Départementales des Bouches-du-Rhône, Annexe d'Aix

Séries B: Parlement

   B3709   Rapport de grains, 1570 jusques à 1670.
   B3710   Rapport sur les grains, 1626–81.
   B3719   Premier cayer du Bureau de la Santé, 6 septembre 1628–20 octobre 1629.
   IVB   Les insinuations, 1598–1700.

Séries E: Notarial Registers

   301E   Fonds Berlie.
   302E   Fonds Bertrand.
   303E   Fonds Lévy-Bram.
   305E   Fonds Vachier.
   306E   Fonds Laucagne.
   307E   Fonds Mouravit.
   308E   Fonds Muraire.
   309E   Fonds Lombard.

Séries H: Hospitals
XXH E3, E4, E5, E6   Hôpital Saint-Jacques.
XXIH E20   Hôpital de la Charité.
XXIIH E1, E2, E3, E4   Hôpital Général de la Miséricorde.
XXVIIIH E2   Oeuvre de la Pureté.
Manuscripts
"Répertoire alphabétique des gradués de l'Université d'Aix, 1531–1791."
5 vols.
Barcilon de Mauvans, Simon-Joseph. "Critique du nobiliaire de Provence
par l'ordre alphabétique." S.D.S.L.
Méchin, Edouard, ed. "L'enseignement en Provence avant la Révolution.
Annales du Collège Royal Bourbon d'Aix depuis les premières dé-
marches faites pour sa fondation jusqu'au 7 Ventose an III époque de
sa suppression. Manuscrits et documents originaux." 4 vols.

Archives Départementales des Bouches-du-Rhône, Marseille
Séries C: Estates of Provence
C40   Verbaux signés, 1658–61
C54   Verbaux signés, 1687–91.
Séries E: Family Papers
XIVE   Fonds Coriolis.
Séries G: Church
G2 498 "Table des principales matières contenues dans les délibérations
prises par le Chapitre de l'Eglise Metropolitaine Saint-Sauveur de la
ville d'Aix et qui ont commencé à être enregistrés le 15e may
1574. . . ."

Archives Communales, Aix-en-Provence
Séries BB: Communal Administration
BB99–BB105   Déliberations du Conseil.
Séries CC: Taxes
CC5–CC6   Registre de Capitation, 1694.
CC7–CC9   Registre de Capitation, 1695.
CC277–CC290   Dettes de la ville.
Séries FF: Police
FF12–FF62   Bureau de Police, déliberations.

Bibliothèque Méjanes, Aix-en-Provence
721–725 (608–612) "Administrations du pays du Provence." 5 vols.
726–732 (822-R.449) "Recueils de pièces sur la Provence." 7 vols.
733 (829-R.449) "Etat et rolle des lettres patentes acquités . . . aux acquéreurs des fiefs de 1626 à 1680."
1133 (R.A. 32) "Jugement de la noblesse de Provence."

1134 (R.A. 32) "Répertoire des jugements de noblesse rendus par les commissaires députés par Sa Majesté, en l'année 1667. . . ."

1143 (630-R.732) Etat du florinage, contenant le revenu noble de tous les fiefs et arrière-fiefs de la province avec les noms des possessuers, fait par M. le Premier Président d'Oppède en 1668."

1144 (1074) "Afflorinement des biens nobles possedez par les seigneurs feudataires de Provence."

"Etat chronologique et heraldique des messires les commissaires du corps de la noblesse de Provence. . . ."

"Etat chronologique et heraldique des messires les syndics du corps de la noblesse de Provence. . . ."

Barcilon de Mauvans, Simon-Joseph. "Critique du nobiliaire de Provence par l'ordre alphabétique."

Musée Arbaud, Aix-en-Provence

452 A1   Beaumont Papers.

1189 A1   Coriolis Papers.

2048 A1   Guiran Papers.

2684 A1   Mazargues Papers.

3823 A1   Séguiran Papers.

Bibliothèque Nationale

Cabinet d'Hozier 33, 181, 310.

Carrés d'Hozier 73, 74, 148, 323, 578.

Nouveau d'Hozier 32.

Published Sources

Blancard, Louis. *Inventaire sommaire des archives départementales des Bouches-du-Rhône.* Séries C. Marseille, 1884–92.

Busquet, Raoul. *Inventaire sommaire des archives départementales des Bouches-du-Rhône.* Séries B. Marseille, 1875–1932.

Clapiers-Collongues, Balthasar de. *Chronologie des officiers des cours souveraines, publiée, annotée, et augmentée par le marquis de Boisgelin.* Aix, 1909–12.

Coste, Jean Paul. *La Ville d'Aix en 1695: Structure urbaine et société.* 2 vols. Aix, 1970.

Grasset, M. Le Comte de. *Inventaire sommaire des archives départementales des Bouches-du-Rhône.* Séries H. *Catalogue des chevaliers de Saint-Jean.* Paris, 1869.

Icard, Séverin. *Armorial de la Provence, du comtat-Venaissin, de la principauté d'Orange, des baronnies du Gapençais, de l'Embrunois, du Briançonnais et comté de Nice.* Marseille, 1932.

Peiresc, Nicolas Claude Fabri de. *Lettres aux frères Dupuy.* Edited by Philippe Tamizey de Larroque. 7 vols. Paris, 1888–98.

Pitton, Jean Scholastique. *Histoire de la ville d'Aix.* . . . Aix, 1666.

Raimbault, Maurice. *Inventaire sommaire des archives communales d'Aix-en-Provence.* Marseille, 1948.

SECONDARY SOURCES

Agulhon, Maurice. *La Vie sociale en Provence intérieure au lendemain de la Révolution.* In *Bibliothèque d'histoire révolutionnaire,* sér. 3, No. 12 (1970).

Allemand, Jeanne. *La Haute Société aixoise dans la seconde moitié du XVIIIe siècle.* Aix, Thèse de droit, 1927.

Artefeuil [pseud.]. *Histoire héroïque et universelle de la noblesse de Provence.* 2 vols. Avignon, 1757.

Aubenas, Roger. "La Famille dans l'ancienne Provence." *Annales d'histoire économique et sociale,* VIII (1936), 532–41.

———. *Le Testament en Provence dans l'ancien droit.* Aix, 1927.

Avenel, Le Vicomte G. de. *La Noblesse Française sous Richelieu.* Paris, 1901.

Baehrel, René. *Une Croissance: La Basse-Provence rurale, fin XVIe siècle–1789.* Paris, 1961.

Baratier, Edouard. *La Démographie provençale du XIIIe au XVIe siècle.* Paris, 1961.

———, ed. *Histoire de Marseille.* Toulouse, 1973.

———, ed. *Histoire de la Provence.* Toulouse, 1969.

———. "Marquisats et comtés en Provence." In *Histoire de la Provence,* edited by Edouard Baratier. Toulouse, 1969.

Baron, Hans. *The Crisis of the Early Italian Renaissance: Civic Humanism and Republican Liberty in an Age of Classicism and Tyranny.* Rev. ed. Princeton, 1966.

Beeler, John. *Warfare in Feudal Europe, 730–1200.* Ithaca, 1971.

Beik, William. *Absolutism and Society in Seventeenth-Century France: State Power and Provincial Aristocracy in Languedoc.* New York, 1985.

Belperron, Pierre. *La Croisade contre les Albigeois et l'union de Languedoc à la France, 1209–1249.* Paris, 1942.

Bitton, Davis. *The French Nobility in Crisis, 1560–1640.* Stanford, 1969.

Blanc, François-Paul. *L'Anoblissement par lettres en Provence à l'époque des réformations de Louis XIV, 1630–1730.* Aix, Thèse de droit, 1971.

———. "Concessions d'armoiries timbrées et anoblissement d'après la jurisprudence provençale moderne." *Provence Historique,* XXV (1975), 525–50.

———. *Origines des familles provençales maintenues dans le second ordre sous le règne de Louis XIV: Dictionnaire généalogique.* Aix, Thèse de droit, 1971.

————. "Un Traité de droit nobiliaire au XVIIe siècle: Alexandre Belleguise et le statut juridique de la noblesse provençale." In *Mélanges Roger Aubenas*. Montpellier, 1974.

Bligny, Bernard, ed. *Histoire du Dauphiné*. Toulouse, 1973.

Bloch, J. R. *L'Anoblissement en France au temps de François Ier*. Paris, 1934.

Bloch, Marc. *Feudal Society*. Translated by L. A. Manyon. Chicago, 1961.

Bohanan, Donna. "The Education of Nobles in Seventeenth-Century Aix-en-Provence." *Journal of Social History*, XX (1987), 757–64.

————. "Matrimonial Strategies Among Nobles of Seventeenth-Century Aix-en-Provence." *Journal of Social History*, XIX (1986), 503–10.

Bonnecorse de Lubières, Gabriel de. *La Condition des gens mariés en Provence aux XIVe, XVe, et XVIe siècles*. Paris, 1929.

Borricaud, René. *Les Hôtels particuliers d'Aix-en-Provence*. Aix, 1971.

Bourde, A. "La Provence baroque, 1596–1660." In *Histoire de la Provence*, edited by Edouard Baratier. Toulouse, 1969.

————. "La Provence au grand siècle." In *Histoire de la Provence*, edited by Edouard Baratier. Toulouse, 1969.

Bourrilly, V. L., and R. Busquet. "Le Moyen-Age, 113–1482." In *Les Bouches-du-Rhône: Encyclopédie départementale*, edited by Paul Masson. Vol. II of 17 vols. Paris, 1913–37.

Boutruche, Robert. *La Crise d'une société: Seigneurs et paysans du Bordelais pendant la Guerre de Cent Ans*. Paris, 1947.

————. *Seigneurie et féodalité*. 2 vols. Paris, 1968.

————. *Une Société provinciale en lutte contre le régime féodal: L'Alleu en Bordelais et en Bazadais du XIe au XVIIIe siècles*. Rodez, 1947.

Brissaud, D. *Les Anglais en Guyenne*. Paris, 1875.

Brucker, Eugene. *Renaissance Florence*. New York, 1969.

Busquet, Raoul. *Histoire des institutions de la Provence de 1482 à 1790*. Marseille, 1920.

Cardin Le Bret, Pierre. *Recherches de noblesse faites en Provence*. Marseille, 1901.

Carrière, Jacqueline. *La Population d'Aix-en-Provence à la fin du XVIIe siècle: Etude de démographie historique d'après le registre de capitation de 1695*. Aix, 1958.

Castillon, H. *Histoire du comté de Foix depuis les temps anciens jusqu'à nos jours*. 2 vols. Toulouse, 1852.

Chartier, Roger, Julia Dominique, and Madeleine Compère. *L'Education en France du XVIe au XVIIIe siècle*. Paris, 1976.

Chaussinand-Nogaret, Guy. *The French Nobility in the Eighteenth Century: From Feudalism to Enlightenment*. Translated by William Doyle. New York, 1985.

Chénon, Emile. *Etude sur l'histoire des alleux en France.* Paris, 1888.

Contamine, Phillipe, ed. *La Noblesse au Moyen-Age, XIe–XVe siècles.* Paris, 1976.

Coriolis, Gaspard H. *Dissertation sur les Etats de Provence.* Aix, 1867.

———. *Traité sur l'administration du comté de Provence.* Aix, 1786.

Coulet, Noel. "Naissance et épanouissement d'une capitale: Aix au Moyen-Age." In *Histoire d'Aix-en-Provence.* Paris, 1977.

Cubells, Monique. "La Politique d'anoblissement de la monarchie en Provence de 1715 à 1789." *Annales du Midi,* XCIV (1982), 173–96.

———. *La Provence des Lumières: Les Parlementaires d'Aix au XVIIIe siècle.* Paris, 1984.

———. "A propos des usurpations de noblesse en Provence sous l'Ancien Régime." *Provence historique,* LXXXII (1970), 224–301.

———. *Structures de groupe et rapports sociaux aux XVIIIe siècle: Les Parlementaires d'Aix-en-Provence.* 5 vols. Aix, Thèse d'Etat, 1980.

Dewald, Jonathan. *The Formation of a Provincial Nobility: The Magistrates of the Parlement of Rouen, 1499–1610.* Princeton, 1980.

Deyon, Pierre. *Amiens, capital provinciale: Etude sur la société urbaine au XVIIe siècle.* Paris, 1967.

———. "A propos des rapports entre la noblesse française et la monarchie absolue pendant la première moitié du XVIIe siècle." *Revue historique,* CCXXXI (1964), 341–56.

Diefendorf, Barbara B. *Paris City Councillors in the Sixteenth Century: The Politics of Patrimony.* Princeton, 1983.

Duby, Georges. "Lineage, Nobility, and Chivalry in the Region of Mâcon During the Twelfth Century." In *Family and Society: Selections from the "Annales: economies, sociétés, civilisations,"* edited by Robert Forster and Orest Ranum. Baltimore, 1976.

———. "Recherches récentes sur la vie rurale en Provence au XIVe siècle." In *Hommes et structures du Moyen-Age,* edited by Georges Duby. Paris, 1973.

———. *La Société aux XIe et XIIe siècles dans la région mâconnaise.* Paris, 1971.

———. "Les Villes du sud-est de la Gaule du VIIIe au XIe siècles." In *Hommes et structures du Moyen-Age,* edited by George Duby. Paris, 1973.

Dupont, A. "L'Evolution sociale du consulat nîmois du milieu du XIIIe au milieu du XVIe siècle." *Annales du Midi,* LXXII (1960), 287–308.

Duprat, E. "Le Haut Moyen-Age." In *Les Bouches-du-Rhône: Encyclopédie départementale,* edited by Paul Masson. Vol. II of 17 vols. Paris, 1913–37.

Durand, Bruno. "Aix: La Vie municipale." In *Les Bouches-du-Rhône: Encyclopédie départementale,* edited by Paul Masson. Vol. XVI of 17 vols. Paris, 1913–37.

————. "Le Rôle des consuls d'Aix dans l'administration du pays." *Provence historique,* VI (1956), 244–59.

Duranti La Calade, Jérôme de. "Aix: L'Evolution Urbaine." In *Les Bouches-du-Rhône: Encyclopédie départementale,* edited by Paul Masson. Vol. XVI of 17 vols. Paris, 1913–37.

Ennen, Edith. *The Medieval Town.* Translated by Natalie Fryde. New York, 1979.

————. "The Different Types of Formation of European Towns." In *Early Medieval Society,* edited by Sylvia Thrupp. New York, 1967.

Fairchilds, Cissie C. *Poverty and Charity in Aix-en-Provence, 1640–1789.* Baltimore, 1976.

Février, Paul-Albert. "Antiquité et haut Moyen-Age: Les Débuts d'une cité." In *Histoire d'Aix-en-Provence.* Paris, 1977.

Flandrin, Jean-Louis. *Families in Former Times: Kinship, Household and Sexuality in Early Modern France.* Translated by Richard Southern. New York, 1979.

Ford, Franklin. *Robe and Sword: The Regrouping of the French Aristocracy After Louis XVI.* Cambridge, Mass., 1953.

Forster, Robert. *The Nobility of Toulouse in the Eighteenth Century: A Social and Economic Study.* Baltimore, 1960.

————. "The Provincial Noble: A Reappraisal." In *American Historical Review,* LXVIII (1962–63), 681–91.

Furet, François, and Jacques Ozouf. *Reading and Writing: Literacy in France from Calvin to Jules Ferry.* New York, 1982.

Gachon, Paul. *Histoire de Languedoc.* Paris, 1921.

Geary, Patrick J. *Aristocracy in Provence: The Rhône Basin at the Dawn of the Carolingian Age.* Philadelphia, 1985.

Genouillac, H. Gourdon de, and the Marquis de Piolenc. *Nobiliaire du département des Bouches-du-Rhône.* Paris, 1863.

Giesey, Ralph. "Rules of Inheritance and Strategies of Nobility in Prerevolutionary France." *American Historical Review,* LXXXII (1977), 271–89.

Goldthwaite, Richard A. *Private Wealth in Renaissance Florence: A Study of Four Families.* Princeton, 1968.

Goubert, Pierre. *The Ancien Régime: French Society, 1600–1750.* Translated by Steve Cox. 2 vols. New York, 1973.

Graff, Harvey J. *The Legacies of Literacy: Continuities and Contradictions in Western Culture.* Bloomington, 1987.

Haitze, Pierre Joseph de. *Histoire de la ville d'Aix, capitale de la Provence.* 6 vols. Aix, 1889.

Hamilton, Earl J. "The Use and Misuse of Price History." *Journal of Economic History,* IV (1944), 47–60.

Harding, Robert. *Anatomy of a Power Elite: The Provincial Governors of Early Modern France.* New Haven, 1978.

Herlihy, David. "Civic Humanism at Pistoia." In *Social and Economic Foundations of the Italian Renaissance,* edited by Anthony Molho. New York, 1969.

————. "Family and Property in Renaissance Florence." In *The Medieval City,* edited by Harry A. Miskimin, David Herlihy, and A. L. Udovitch. New Haven, 1977.

————. *Medieval and Renaissance Pistoia: The Social History of an Italian Town, 1200–1450.* New Haven, 1967.

Hexter, J. H. *Reappraisals in History: New Views of History and Society in Early Modern Europe.* New York, 1961.

Higounet, Charles. *Le Comté de Comminges de ses origines à son annexion à la couronne.* 2 vols. Paris, 1949.

————. "Le Groupe aristocratique en Aquitaine et en Gascogne, fin Xe–début XIIe siècle." In *Les structures sociales de l'Aquitaine, du Languedoc, et de l'Espagne au premier âge féodal.* Toulouse, 1968.

————. *Histoire de l'Aquitaine.* Toulouse, 1971.

Holt, Mack P. Introduction to *Society and Institutions in Early Modern France,* edited by Mack P. Holt. Athens, Ga., 1991.

Houston, R. A. *Literacy in Early Modern Europe: Culture and Education, 1500–1800.* London, 1988.

Huppert, George. *Les Bourgeois Gentilshommes: An Essay on the Definition of Elites in Renaissance France.* Chicago, 1977.

————. *Public Schools in Renaissance France.* Chicago, 1984.

Kettering, Sharon. *Judicial Politics and Urban Revolt in Seventeenth-Century France: The Parlement of Aix, 1629–1659.* Princeton, 1978.

————. "Patronage and Politics During the Fronde." *French Historical Studies,* XIV (1986), 409–46.

————. *Patrons, Brokers, and Clients in Seventeenth-Century France.* New York, 1986.

Leage, R. W. *Roman Private Law.* London, 1948.

Lepointe, Gabriel. *Droit romain et ancien droit français: Régimes matrimoniaux, liberalités, successions.* Paris, 1958.

————. *Histoire des institutions et des faits sociaux (987–1875).* Paris, 1956.

Le Roy Ladurie, Emmanuel. *Les Paysans de Languedoc.* 2 vols. Paris, 1969.

————. "Family Structures and Inheritance Customs in Sixteenth-Century France." In *Family and Inheritance: Rural Society in Western Europe, 1200–1800,* edited by Jack Goody, Joan Thirsk, and E. P. Thompson. New York, 1976, pp. 37–70.

Lewis, Archibald R. *The Development of Southern French and Catalan Society, 718–1050.* Austin, 1965.

———. "La Féodalite dans le Toulousain et la France méridionale, 850–1050." *Annales du Midi*, LXXV (1964), 247–59.

Lodge, Eleanor C. "Edward I and His Tenants-in-Chief." *Transactions of the Royal Historical Society*, Ser. 4, VII (1924), 1–26.

———. *Gascony Under English Rule*. London, 1926.

Loirette, François. "The Defense of the Allodium in Seventeenth-Century Agenais: An Episode in the Local Resistance to Encroaching Royal Power." In *State and Society in Seventeenth-Century France*, edited by Raymond F. Kierstead. New York, 1975.

Lougee, Carolyn C. *Le Paradis des Femmes: Women, Salons, and Social Stratification in Seventeenth-Century France*. Princeton, 1976.

Magendie, M. *La Politesse mondaine et les théories de l'honnêteté, en France au XVIIe siècle, de 1600 à 1700*. 2 vols. Paris, 1925.

Magnou-Nortier, Elisabeth. "Fidelité et féodalité méridionales d'après les serments de fidelité, Xe–début XIIe siècle." In *Les structures sociales du l'Aquitaine, du Languedoc et de l'Espagne au premier âge féodal*. Toulouse, 1968.

Major, J. Russell. "The Crown and the Aristocracy in Renaissance France." *American Historical Review*, LXIX (1964), 631–45.

———. "Noble Income, Inflation, and the Wars of Religion in France." *American Historical Review*, LXXXVI (1981), 21–48.

———. "The Renaissance Monarchy: A Contribution to the Periodization of History." *Emory University Review*, XIII (1957), 112–24.

———. *Representative Government in Early Modern France*. New Haven, 1980.

Maza, Sarah C. *Servants and Masters in Eighteenth-Century France: The Uses of Loyalty*. Princeton, 1983.

Meyer, Jean. *La Noblesse bretonne au XVIIIe siècle*. 2 vols. Paris, 1966.

Mousnier, Roland. "L'Evolution des institutions monarchiques en France et ses relations avec l'état social." *XVIIe Siècle*, LVIII–LIX (1963), 55–72.

———. *The Institutions of France Under the Absolute Monarchy, 1598–1789*. Translated by Brian Pearce. 2 vols. Chicago, 1979.

———. Introduction to *Problèmes de stratifications sociale: Deux cahiers de la noblesse pour les Etats-Généraux de 1649–1651*, edited by R. Mousnier, J. P. Labatut, and Y. Durand. Paris, 1965.

———. *La Venalité des offices sous Henri IV et Louis XIII*. 2d ed. Paris, 1971.

Mumford, Lewis. *The City in History*. New York, 1961.

Mundy, John H., and Peter Riesenberg. *The Medieval Town*. Princeton, 1958.

Nicholas, Barry. *An Introduction to Roman Law*. Ppr. New York, 1962.

Nicolas, C. *Tableau comparatif des poids et mesures anciennes du département des Bouches-du-Rhône avec les poids et mesures républicaines* . . . . Aix, 1910.

Norberg, Kathryn. *Rich and Poor in Grenoble, 1600–1814*. Berkeley, 1985.

Nordhaus, John David. *Arma et Litterae: The Education of the Noblesse de Race in Sixteenth-Century France.* Microfilm. Ann Arbor, 1974.

Ourliac, Paul. "La Droit privé dans les villes du Midi de la France." *Recueils de la Société Jean Bodin,* VIII (1957).

————— and J. de Malafosse. *Histoire de droit privé.* 3 vols. Paris, 1961.

Pearl, Jonathan L. *Guise and Provence: Political Conflict in the Epoch of Richelieu.* Microfilm. Ann Arbor, 1968.

Perroy, Edouard. "Social Mobility Among the French *Noblesse* in the Later Middle Ages." *Past and Present,* XXI (1962), 25–38.

Pillorget, René. "Un Document concernant la peste et l'insurrection d'Aix (1630)." *Revue de la Méditerranée,* XXI (1961), 209–21.

—————. "The *Cascaveoux:* The Insurrection at Aix of the Autumn of 1630." In *State and Society in Seventeenth-Century France,* edited by Raymond Kirstead. New York, 1975.

—————. *Les Mouvements insurrectionnels de Provence entre 1596 et 1715.* Paris, 1975.

Pirenne, Henri. *Medieval Cities: Their Origins and the Revival of Trade.* Translated by Frank D. Halsey. Princeton, 1946.

Poly, Jean-Pierre, and Eric Bournazel. *La Mutation féodale.* Paris, 1980.

Poumarède, Jacques. *Les Successions dans le sud-ouest de la France au Moyen-Age.* Paris, 1972.

Ranum, Orest. "Comment on Session: Social and Urban Aspects of the Grand Siècle." *Proceedings of the Western Society for French History,* XI (1984), 61–64.

Rashdall, Hastings. *The Universities of Europe in the Middle Ages.* 3 vols. Oxford, Eng., 1895.

Ribbe, Charles de. *Les Familles et la société en France avant la Révolution, d'après des documents originaux.* Paris, 1873.

—————. *La Société provençale à la fin du Moyen-Age.* Paris, 1898.

Roebuck, Janet. *The Shaping of Urban Society: A History of City Forms and Function.* New York, 1974.

Romier, Lucien. *Le Royaume de Catherine de Médicis.* 2 vols. Paris, 1922.

Rostovtzeff, Michael I. *A History of the Ancient World.* Translated by J. D. Duff. 2 vols. New York, 1945.

Roupnel, Gaston. *La Ville et la campagne au XVIIe siècle: Etude sur les populations du pays dijonnais.* Paris, 1955.

Roure, Le Baron du. *Les Recherches de noblesse en Provence sous Louis XIV et Louis XV.* Paris, 1910.

Sabaratier, Nicole. *L'Hôpital Saint-Jacques d'Aix-en-Provence, 1519–1789.* Aix, Thèse du Droit, 1964.

Sagnac, Phillippe. *La Formation de la société française moderne.* 2 vols. Paris, 1945.

Salmon, J. H. M. "Storm over the Noblesse." *Journal of Modern History*, LIII (1981), 242–57.

Sautel, Gérard. *Le Bureau de Police d'Aix-en-Provence: Une Jurisdiction municipale de police sous l'Ancien Régime*. Paris, 1946.

————. "Les Villes du Midi méditerranéen au Moyen-Age: Aspects économiques et sociaux, IXe–XIIIe siècles." *Recueils de la Société Jean Bodin*, Vol. VII, Pt. 2 (1955).

Schalk, Ellery. *From Valor to Pedigree: Ideas of Nobility in France in the Sixteenth and Seventeenth Centuries*. Princeton, 1986.

————. "Nobility, Elites, and Absolutism in Marseille in the Sixteenth and Seventeenth Centuries." Paper presented at annual meeting of the Western Society for French History, New Orleans, 1989.

Sée, Henri. *Les Classes rurales et le régime domanial en France au Moyen-Age*. Paris, 1901.

Sherman, Charles Phineas. *Roman Law in the Modern World*. 3 vols. New York, 1924.

Stone, Lawrence. "The Educational Revolution in England, 1560–1640." *Past and Present*, XXVIII (1964), 41–80.

————. *The Family, Sex, and Marriage in England, 1500–1800*. New York, 1977.

Thirsk, Joan. "The European Debate on Customs of Inheritance, 1500–1700." In *Family and Inheritance: Rural Society in Western Europe, 1200–1800*, edited by Jack Goody, Joan Thirsk, and E. P. Thompson. New York, 1976, pp. 177–96.

Timbal, Pierre-Clement. "Les Villes du consulat dans le Midi de la France." In *Recueils de la Société Jean Bodin*, VI (1954), 343–70.

Traer, James. *Marriage and the Family in Eighteenth-Century France*. Ithaca, 1980.

Vaissière, Pierre de. *Gentilshommes campagnards de l'ancienne France*. Paris, 1925.

Vovelle, Michel. "Apogée ou déclin d'une capitale provinciale: Le XVIIIe siècle." In *Histoire d'Aix-en-Provence*. Paris, 1977.

————. *Piété baroque et déchristianisation en Provence au XVIIIe siècle*. Paris, 1973.

Wiley, W. L. *The Gentlemen of Renaissance France*. Cambridge, Mass., 1954.

Wood, James B. *The Nobility of the Election of Bayeux, 1463–1666: Continuity Through Change*. Princeton, 1980.

————. "The Decline of the Nobility of Sixteenth- and Early Seventeenth-Century France: Myth or Reality?" *Journal of Modern History*, XLVIII (1967), supplement.

Woodward, William Harrison. *Studies in Education During the Age of the Renaissance, 1400–1600*. Cambridge, Eng., 1906.

Wolfe, Philippe. *Histoire du Languedoc*. Toulouse, 1967.

Wolff, Louis. *La Vie des parlementaires provençaux au XVIe siècle*. Marseille, 1924.

————. *Histoire du Languedoc*. Toulouse, 1967.

Yver, Jean. *Egalité entre héritiers et exclusion des enfants dotés: Essai de géographie coutumière*. Paris, 1966.

Zeller, Gaston. *Les Institutions de la France au XVIe siècle*. Paris, 1948.

INDEX